"Did You See My Ad?"

When, Why and How to Advertise the Small Business

Larry Semon

BRICK HOUSE PUBLISHING COMPANY
Andover, Massachusetts

To the profession of advertising
which has given me the most
rewarding years of my life, and

To Dirk
who made this a better book.

Library of Congress Cataloging-in-Publication Data

Semon, Larry. 1922-
"Did you see my ad?": when, why, and how to
advertise the small business/Larry Semon.
p. cm.
Includes index.
ISBN 0-931790-78-6 (pbk.)
1. Advertising 2. Small business. I. Title.
HF5823.S466 1988 88-6990
659.1—dc19 CIP

Contents

1 Advertising: Tool for Profit   1

2 Advertising Can Sell Anything   4

3 Two Rules of Research   7

4 Advertising versus Public Relations   11

5 What About Using an Advertising Agency?   20

6 The Media as Your Agency   26

7 How Newspaper Advertising Gets Done   32

8 All About Radio and Television Advertising   49

9 Direct Response Advertising   63

10 Direct Mail Advertising   67

11 Co-op Advertising   78

12 The Yellow Pages   80

13 Transit Advertising   85

14 "Free" Advertising   88

15 Your Advertising Budget   91

16 Creative Concepts for Success   97

17 "Did You See My Ad?"   105

18 Let's Write an Ad!   108

19 The Ten Commandments   116

Index   121

1

Advertising: Tool for Profit

Every day of the year, people who want to sell something use a marketing tool called "advertising." Perhaps they run an ad in a local penny-saver (a free newspaper) which costs them nothing, or they run an ad in the classified section of their leading newspaper, which might cost ten dollars. Perhaps they put their ad on the back cover of TV GUIDE, and pay more than $100,000 to do that just once.

All advertisers rank somewhere between those extremes, but they all want to achieve the same goal: *Move the merchandise out—take the money in!*

The goal of this book is to enable any owner or manager of a small business to develop and place his own advertising inexpensively and effectively. That's a big job for a small book because every day thousands of dollars are wasted by people who learn too late that their advertising was not successful in gathering customers.

The Advertising Manager of one of the largest companies in the world is quoted as saying, "I am convinced that a sizable portion of our multi-million-dollar annual advertising budget is wasted! If only I knew which part!"

Advertising is an art, not a science. There is no mathematical or chemical formula for success. All rules—even those stated flatly in this book—are made to be broken. But, as in any art, the true professional knows the rules before choosing to break them. At least know for sure you are taking a chance by doing something that has been proven time and again to be ineffective. Then, if you still have reason to do it, go ahead. You may be successful or you may be one more person who has learned that basic advertising rules should generally be followed. This is particularly true for the inexperienced and even more true for anyone working on a small budget. You cannot afford to waste your dollars in the hope that your rule-breaking approach might pay off.

Stick to the rules, at least in the beginning. Become an advertising trailblazer when you're rich and can afford failure. If you budget the expenses of your business operation in the way most often recommended, you will be spending about the same number of dollars for advertising that you spend for your rent, which is about ten to fifteen percent of the total income from your business. Even if you spend only half that amount, you must be sure every penny spent in advertising is working as hard for you as possible. Actually, the less money you invest in advertising, the more it becomes vital that each penny is wisely spent.

If you intend to operate a service or retail business without advertising of some kind, you might as well run in a marathon with one leg. If you believe you can "save money" by not advertising, you are making a tragic mistake. You are not taking every advantage of the great tool available to you to build sales to the maximum. You will be ignoring your competition. If they advertise and you do not, they will be the business that gathers new customers—some of whom will be yours!

More than one multi-million dollar company has taken the attitude they didn't need advertising because they had little or no competition. Without exception their sales suffered tremendously. In some cases, they went out of business. They faded from public view because the public did not know they were in the marketplace. The Proctor and Gamble Company markets everything from soap to baby diapers to coffee. Their advertising budget for all products is probably more than $200 million a year! They don't do it because it is fun to spend money and they don't do it because they like to see their name in print. They do it to fight the competition. In most product categories, they sell more than their competition does.

Advertising is a marketing tool. If you operate a hardware store, you know that the best carpenters not only buy tools, they buy the best tools for the job they have to do. You must do the same thing if you want to lead your competition in sales. You must advertise.

Equally important, you must do it right. You can't spend money just for the pleasure of seeing your name in print. Your advertising must work and work hard! So, if you're going to advertise, learn how to do it to get the most for your buck. Learn the language. Learn the rules, and then

Go for it!

2

Advertising
Can Sell Anything

Not true. It might be true that a poorly designed, badly
written ad, or one placed on the wrong day or wrong page
can deliver **some** sales. But it probably won't be worth the
investment.

"A/S ratio" is a classy marketing term that simply means
advertising to sales ratio. Translation: What did it cost you
to advertise? If you spend $500 for an ad to move $1,000
worth of merchandise, you have an inefficient A/S ratio of
50%. No small business can affort a 50% A/S ratio, no
matter how much business it does. Other expenses such as
rent, staff, salaries, and product cost almost always account
for more than the remaining 50%—so where's the profit?

Another thing advertising cannot do is generate repeat
sales for a product that isn't worth the money, or for a
product that can be had elsewhere for less money. You
might tempt the public once, but they won't be back. Most
likely they won't come back for any product you advertise,
either.

Everything about your business must contribute to the
sale. The product must be as good as the public can get
elsewhere for the same or less money. Your location should
be convenient. Your decor and housekeeping should be
attractive, if simple. Your staff should be knowledgeable and
friendly enough to make customers happy.

All of these things add up to the magic achievement of **marketing**. Advertising is only a part of marketing. Don't ask advertising to do everything to generate sales. But make sure it does what it **can** do.

So important are these other marketing considerations that it is very tempting to concentrate on them for your benefit, although this book is supposed to be concerned only with advertising. There's good reason for that temptation. Advertising alone will not do a **long-term** job of building sales if other marketing advantages are not maximized. Advertising can and will get you new customers, but advertising will not get **repeat** business and it will not get you referrals **unless** the experience of buying from you has been a good one.

If you rely on new customers alone to build your business, your sales will not grow. In fact, your advertising will pay off less and less because it will be bucking bad word-of-mouth. If that happens, you may blame your advertising. Don't. It's not your advertising's fault. It's yours.

Advertising can create interest in your product or service. Advertising alone will not sell it. How many times have you seen a newspaper or television ad or heard a radio commercial which makes you want to buy, but when you get to the store, they're out of it? Or it isn't what you thought it would be? Or you can't find someone to wait on you?

Everyone has had one or more of these experiences, and they are a marketing tragedy. Advertising has done its job. It has delivered a customer to the store in a buying mood. You may still fail to make a sale because the second half of the job—the selling—has not been done.

Don't become an advertising success and a marketing failure. The only thing you could do worse than that is to blame advertising for your lack of success.

"My competition doesn't advertise. Why should I?" This is a common and dangerous attitude. Think about it for a moment. If you were a salesman, doing no better and no worse than your fellow salesmen in the same company, would you take the attitude that there is not point in trying to do better? Of course not—especially if you were on a commission-only basis. You would try to do better no matter what anyone else was doing. Just because "no one else is doing it" is no reason for you not to grow!

Most prominent of those with the attitude that their particular business does not need advertising are local service companies, including gas stations, drycleaners, hardware stores and hair-styling salons. The latter group is going through a minor revolution. Large, franchised hair salon chains **are** advertising and what is happening? They are taking business away from local shops and driving some small, independent salons out of business.

The franchised salons do not generally have better equipment, better surroundings, better locations or better operators. They are advertising impressively. In many cases, they are not even less expensive than the small local salon, but the small local salon does not advertise, and the result is that the big birds are getting all the worms.

It can almost be guaranteed that if you are the **only** business of your kind in your neighborhood who is advertising, you are going to get most of the business! That's a strong claim, but is has proven to be accurate time after time. The purpose of advertising is to deliver customers to your door rather than to the doors of your competitors.

If you are one of the many small businesses who do not advertise, you will find when you do start that your neighborhood has many potential customers who never even knew you were so conveniently nearby. You will find it difficult to believe that someone who lives a block or two from your store never thought to do business with you, but you will have that experience time after time. Even better, people will travel from other neighborhoods to buy from you because they have had a bad experience in their own neighborhood and were led to you by your advertising!

3

Two Rules of Research

"I can write a better ad than that!" Maybe you can. You would not be the first non-professional advertising writer to come up with copy that moves buyers to buy—but the likelihood is not great. Many of the ads we all say we hate (particularly ones we see on television) have been history-making in their ability to sell.

Years ago, Anacin ran a television commercial featuring an actor with simulated headache pain in the form of animated hammer pounding, lightning striking and other distasteful events. Many members of the general public said they disliked the commercial, but Anacin began to outsell other headache remedies as a result. The lesson is clear: an ad people dislike can sell.

Before an advertising agency runs an ad in a newspaper or magazine or on television, they usually test the copy beforehand, to find the answers to the following two questions:

Will anyone pay attention to the advertisement?
Will the advertisement convince anyone to buy the product?

If an automobile manufacturer, for example, is going to spend a million dollars or more running a commercial on television, he wants to know that his message will sell cars or trucks.

The problem is that copy research, like advertising itself, is an art. History has shown that copy research can be disastrously misleading. It can indicate that an ad will move merchandise but the ad fails. It can indicate that an ad is ineffective and the result will be success.

A case in point often cited is that of the Edsel automobile, on which the Ford Motor Company spent a fortune in market research. The researchers concluded that the car would be an instant success. The car was a total failure, and millions of dollars were lost in trying to get the public to buy a car that research said they wanted, but which they rejected in the showroom.

As the advertiser of a small business, you won't be in the market to buy expensive copy research. You'll simply prepare your ad and run it. Either the customers will appear magically or they won't. That's your "research."

Be prepared for disappointment. If you prepare an ad that says exactly what you want to tell the public about your product or service and nobody comes to buy, it may or may not be the fault of the ad.

The product or service itself may be unimpressive. Actually, this doesn't happen as often as you might think. Eskimos **do** buy refrigerators. At least the ones who live in houses do. If you have faith in the value of your product or service, you are probably not alone.

Most likely, you have failed in one of two ways (or both).

1. You have failed to state clearly and simply the advantages of what you are offering: Price. Quality. Convenience. Exclusivity. Reliability. Reputation. These are all **vital** copy points. Some may be more applicable to your business than others, but they each give the public a **reason** to do business with you rather than with the competition. Pick the most outstanding advantages you have to offer over your competition. Perhaps there is only one. That's all you really need if it is impressive enough. Resist the

temptation to give your total sales pitch in one ad. That approach will most often fail.

2. You have not reached your target audience. Example: Do not run at ten a.m. a radio or television commercial appealing to teenagers. Why? They're all in school except those with the flu or playing hooky. You are not reaching your target audience. Another truism for reaching teenagers: They don't read newspapers. Their mothers do, though. So maybe you want to try to sell Mama and let **her** buy it for her teenager. (This can be dangerous because you are asking Mama to be your salesman, and she is just as liable to kill the sale as help you make it.)

If you want to reach teenagers on radio or television, the first time segment you should try is 3 to 7 p.m. After 7 p.m. too many of them are watching network television, doing homework, or out on a date. Also, the cost of television time is highest between 7 and 11 p.m. That's Prime Time, and so is the cost. On radio, the most expensive time is 7 to 9 a.m. and 5 to 7 p.m. It's called Drive Time, when commuters are listening on their car radios, and you'll pay dearly for it without necessarily reaching the people you most want to reach.

So, you can learn two things from research without spending a nickel:

1. Don't overwhelm your audience with every sales point you can think of. It's just too much work for people to read or listen to or watch on television. Tell them just enough to get them into the store and do your selling there. This rule applies to almost anything you do in the way of communicating with potential customers. (The single exception to this might be in direct mail advertising, discussed in the chapter on direct mail.) Readers, listeners and watchers of newspapers, radio and television have been brought up with a mental "switch" that can turn off when advertising begins. You must

GET THEIR ATTENTION
MAKE THEM AN OFFER THEY CAN'T REFUSE
THEN SHUT UP!

If you have not focused your effort in these ways, your advertising will fail no matter how loud or long you talk.

2. Reach your target audience. If you're going to sell a pizza parlor on radio, a pop music station will reach more of your target audience than the classical music station will. It may be true that Cadillac owners eat pizza, but they are not really your target. Know your target!

Many large advertisers spend hundreds of thousands of dollars on research to learn that what they **thought** was the most impressive offer in their ad won't even be **noticed** by the public! The advertiser was talking to himself.

If you want to make more than one claim in your ad such as price and guarantee, you will be doing what advertising writers call "multi-claim" advertising. It can be done successfully. But emphasize only one of the claims in your ad. And make sure it is not the same claim your competition is making. The public won't remember where they read it or which store made the claim.

A leading furniture store retailer in a large city is currently running a television commercial promoting recliners. The public already has a pretty good idea that his prices are among the lowest in town. His previous advertising has always featured price. So what he talks about in his television commercial is that he offers a huge selection—more than anyone else! He doesn't even mention price, although price is the biggest single reason for his great success!

That's what is meant about making one claim—and then shutting up!

4

Advertising versus Public Relations

A simple definition of the difference between advertising and public relations is that you pay for advertising and public relations is free.

Don't you believe it. You pay for public relations and often through the nose. A favorable mention about your restaurant or clothing store by a popular newspaper columnist is very hard to come by. After all, the columnist's first job is to write an interesting column, not to promote your business. So, don't telephone him with the thrilling news that you are going to give a discount on all hamburgers next weekend. If a sports superstar is going to visit your store the columnist may print it, but an Anniversary Sale in your store means little to him or his readers.

A successful public relations program is the achievement of highly skilled professionals who can get news about your business into print. They can achieve this even when the news is not earth-shaking, and they will charge you a lot of money to do it.

Most often, public relations firms charge just the make the effort. They almost never guarantee that it will actually be accomplished. Even worse, if the public relations firm is hot enough to really provide success in spreading the good word about your store or service, they often don't want to represent a small business. Or they quote such a large fee for their services you will be discouraged from hiring them. They just can't make enough money from the assignment of serving you. Generally, therefore, public relations firms are not usable by a small business.

PUBLIC RELATIONS YOU CAN DO FOR YOURSELF

Your public relations should be concentrated on making your customers so pleased with your products or services that they recommend you to their friends. Remember that just **one** unhappy customer can cost you ten more customers by bad-mouthing you to his or her friends. On the other hand, you cannot depend on one happy customer to deliver ten new customers to you. But, if each customer—or even one out of two—delivers you one new customer, you will grow in sales daily. Ask every customer, "How did you hear about us?" If you can pin it down to a referral by another customer, telephone the customer who recommended you. Thank him or her and offer some small reward (discount or gift) for having recommended you.

This takes time, but it will build your customer list. Give your business cards out with each sale, and ask your customers to give the cards to their friends. You'll be surprised how many of them will be glad to do that— particularly if they are told there will be a reward in it for them.

Accept exchanges and refunds if you can do it without severe financial loss. Don't charge for that hamburger if the customer complains. Of course, you'll learn quickly not to be taken in by hustlers. But keeping every customer as happy as possible will keep that customer coming back and encourage him or her to recommend you.

There are things you can do yourself without the aid of a public relations expert. Newspapers and even local magazines usually feature a column promoting local services. For example:

RESTAURANT GUIDE
HANDY-ANDY (HOME REPAIR)
FINANCIAL
REAL ESTATE
RETAIL (FASHION) NEWS
AUTO NEWS

These columns appear in your local newspaper(s) once a week or more. What you should do is to prepare a press release and mail it to the writer of the column. As mentioned, the writer of a **news** column may not be too interested in the opening of your new pizza parlor, but the writers of the service columns depend on people like you providing them with information for their columns.

The press release you write should be **no more than one page**. As in any copy you prepare, don't try to tell the story of your life! Make it brief, and write short sentences which tell the reader quickly and easily what you've got. Columnists don't want to rewrite your copy. If it is too long or confusing, it'll be filed in the wastebasket.

Attach a **short** note to the front of your press release telling the columnist that you'd welcome a visit. The columnist probably won't come, but if you have a product or service he can use, give him a "freebie" and watch how quickly your press release gets published.

After you've written your press release, read it over and pretend **you** are the columnist when you read it. If there is one sentence in the release that makes you say, "Who cares?" **eliminate it**. That's called editing and it's more important than writing.

On the next pages, I've provided a sample press release and the cover note that goes with it. The press release you write should be no longer than the sample. The best guide to how much information to offer is the column where you want it to appear. If the writer of the column usually provides 100 words, your press release should be no longer.

If the writer of the column wants more information, he'll call you to ask for it.

As in tennis or golf, follow through is very important. What is it? The day after your press release should have been delivered to the columnist, phone her/him. Introduce yourself politely and ask **only** two questions:

> Did you receive our press release?
> Is there any more information I might give you?

Do not ask if the columnist is going to publish it! That question only puts him on the spot and he won't like it. Just try to make the columnist's job easier. That is really all anyone wants.

If the columnist does publish your release, write a thank-you note. Make it no more than one or two sentences:

October 10, 1988

Dear Ms. Jones:

We at ANDY'S PIZZA PARLOR were very glad for the mention you gave us in your column.

We never miss reading your column and we were proud to be a part of it today.

Sincerely,

ANDY'S PIZZA PARLOR

This may seem of slight importance, but it's not—and almost nobody does it! (How many thank-you notes do you receive when you do a favor for someone?) Just writing a thank-you note has been known to get **another** mention. And after all, it's only good manners.

What if you have more than one newspaper in your area? Do you send the press release to all papers? Of course, you do. What do you care if three papers print the same press release the same day? It won't hurt you, and besides it is not likely that it will happen. Send the press release to everyone you can think of.

Now let's take a look at the sample press release and the cover note that goes with it. The cover note should be **smaller** than the press release and should be attached to the front of the release. It should have the appearance of a "buck slip."

Dear Ms. Jones:

We at ANDY'S PIZZA PARLOR are fans of your column—we never miss it.

We're beginning an ambitious delivery program on November first, as explained in the enclosed press release.

We hope you might be able to use this item in your column.

ANDY'S PIZZA PARLOR

Here is a sample press release:

FOR IMMEDIATE RELEASE

ANDY'S PIZZA PARLOR at 3535 Clairemont Drive has been a neighborhood favorite since 1970. ANDY'S features pizza in three different sizes, with a variety of toppings, that range in price from $5.95.

Starting November 1st, ANDY'S will provide FREE DELIVERY SERVICE in the Clairemont area. The free delivery service applies to any purchase, and here's the big news: ANDY'S guarantees delivery within 30 minutes or your order is FREE!

So the next time you think PIZZA, think ANDY'S. Call ANDY'S PIZZA at 276-4540 for free delivery.

Do you see anything wrong with the public relations release you've just read? If not, read it again. Is the most important information presented **first**? No. It is in the second paragraph. That's wrong. It makes the release look like an ad and the writer of the column will resent (and maybe not use) it.

What if you **reverse** the order of those two paragraphs? If you do, it will provide the reader with the important information promptly.

A Creative Writing course instructor might try to teach you to set the reader up for important information with some "color" in the first paragraph. Basic newspaper writing teaches you to put the important facts in the first paragraph. The following paragraphs provide details of each fact presented in the first paragraph. That technique remains the most effective way of telling any informational story.

So—let's reverse our paragraphs and see what we've got:

FOR IMMEDIATE RELEASE

Starting November 1st, ANDY'S PIZZA PARLOR will provide FREE DELIVERY SERVICE in the Clairemont area.   The free delivery service applies to any purchase, and here's the big news: ANDY'S guarantees delivery within 30 minutes or your order is FREE!

ANDY'S PIZZA PARLOR at 3535 Clairemont Drive has been a neighborhood favorite since 1970. ANDY'S features pizza in three different sizes, with a variety of toppings, that range in price from $5.95.

So the next time you think pizza, think ANDY'S.   Call ANDY'S PIZZA at 276-4540 for free delivery .

MORE PUBLIC RELATIONS YOU CAN DO
FOR YOURSELF

In every city there are public service organizations dedicated to raising money for some disadvantaged group. Typical would be the Red Cross or the Boy Scouts or United Way.

These very large organizations are difficult to tie in with because they do not have the time or the staff to work with anyone other than "big guns" who can help them gather big dollars. But there are plenty of smaller public service organizations such as Neighborhood Watch or senior citizens groups, women's clubs, the YMCA, the YWCA, etc., who might be very glad to work with you to help them gather support for their cause.

Whenever you can work with any of these people, you have the opportunity to gather new customers from two sources. First, from the members of the organization itself because they get to know you and like you. Second, from all the neighborhood people you meet through the promotion.

What is the promotion?

Run a contest! Contests are terrific promotions. (Most of us are still waiting to win our $10 million from Publishers' Clearing House.) The participation of the public in contests is enormous. That's why they're still being done by so many big marketers.

Contact the public service organizations in your neighborhood and offer to work with them on a promotion. They'll be glad to hear from you in most cases. Your participation will be merch-andise or service from your business. Sure, it will cost you but not a lot and your prestige in the community will benefit as well as your cash register.

You should be able to do at least four promotions a year with the public service organizations in your city. Look up CLUBS in your Yellow Pages and contact the ones that seem likely tie-ins with your business or service. You might also call the Chamber of Commerce (or visit them) and tell them you want to contact all the service clubs in your neighborhood. Ask them if they have a listing of the kind of people you want to contact. The Chamber of Commerce is there to help you. Use it.

RADIO AND TELEVISION PROMOTIONS

Call the public service departments of your local radio and television stations. They are hungry for help in their programming. There may not be a "department" but there will be a person who handles public service for the station and they will be glad to help you put together a promotion with a local service organization which the station will advertise as part of its service to the community.

Most cities have at least one local television station which does "Do It Yourself" demonstrations as part of a program. They need guests as badly as Johnny Carson does. Of course, they won't pay you to be on their program and be interviewed by their host but you can get some great PR from such appearances.

Businesses which are naturals for demonstration on television include restaurants, florists, beauty parlors, retail fashion stores, and more. Even something as left field as a radio/television repair store can give a demonstration of how to avoid costly repairs. Don't assume they won't want you.

These public relations efforts are exactly what a large public relations firm would charge you for putting together. You can do it yourself. All you have to do is try. And don't be discouraged by getting turned down. Just move on to the next station and repeat your offer.

5

What About Using
an Advertising Agency?

Let's be sure you know what an advertising agency is and does. An advertising agency accepts the assignment of preparing your advertising and placing it with the media, after you approve:

1. How much money you are going to spend on a weekly, monthly or yearly basis. They plan the best way to spend your budget for a given period of time. They should also counsel you on how much or how little money you should spend to combat the competition.

2. How that budget is going to be divided among newspapers, radio, television, magazines, catalogs, direct mail, etc.

3. The copy approaches that will be used, and the preparation of the copy itself—the newspaper ad or the radio or television commercial—so the medium can use it.

HOW AN ADVERTISING AGENCY GETS PAID

Advertising agencies do other things for their clients. They receive all the bills from the various media and pass them along to you. You pay the agency and the agency pays the media, after deducting their commission from what you have paid them.

Even if you are not new, if you are a small business and don't have an impressive financial statement showing lots of money in the bank, the agency often asks for two things: cash with order and a retainer.

Cash with order: This means that when the agency places an order for $500 worth of radio spots, you will pay for the spots before they go on the air. This is normal practice, and if you think about it, you won't be offended by such a request. When an agency places your order for advertising with a newspaper or a radio station or anyone else, the agency becomes a part of your contract with the media. If the media isn't paid, they will go after the agency *first* for the money.

Most newspapers but few radio or television stations offer a discount for prompt payment of bills. It is customary to pass this discount on to you. If you have earned it by paying cash with order, you should get it. Agencies have been known not to offer it, and if you don't ask you don't get!

Retainer: An agency cannot charge you cash with order for the *preparation* of your ads or commercials because they won't know in advance what the exact costs will be. They can only estimate. So you pay a retainer when you hire the agency, not much different from a rent deposit on an apartment. The retainer makes certain that any costs the agency has incurred on your behalf in preparing advertising material will be paid. If you should suddenly drop your agency or go out of business, your account with the agency can be settled from the retainer.

Unfortunately, it can give the agency an opportunity to take advantage of you. The agency may want to charge you for some service you thought would be free and the fight is on.

Let's say you and your agency agree on a copy approach and the agency writes the ad along those lines. What if you don't like the ad and the agency accepts the chore of rewriting? Some agencies will charge you for every piece of copy written and for every layout that their art department draws!   Others will go along with your demands for revisions without making a charge. Some agencies charge a client for every single phone call the client makes to them, much as some lawyers do. Others don't.

A retainer is also a guarantee that the agency will make some money from your account, should you suddenly discontinue advertising. Usually, the entire retainer is kept by the agency if you fail to spend the advertising dollars you have agreed to spend in a specified time period—usually six months or a year.

An agency of any stature is usually suspicious of small accounts and often with good reason. If you are spending $1,000 a week for advertising, you are spending at the rate of $50,000 for the year. That's a lot of money out of your pocket but the agency only makes 15% of that, or $7,500 for the year. They are going to give you only so much of their time for the weekly $144 they earn from your account. You tend to feel you are spending a fortune with them and they tend to feel they are not making enough money from your account. Not a formula for a friendly relationship.

Generally, all preparation charges are billed to you at cost plus agency commission. If the agency pays a photographer $100 for a photo to be used in your ad, the agency will charge you the same amount for the photo. It is normal business practice for the agency to add 15% of the cost to that bill as their commission.   They have earned it by supplying a photographer who will deliver a worthwhile photo for your ad.

The same philosophy holds true for the cost of actors or announcers in your radio or television commercial.   The agency assumes the responsibility of finding an actor they (and you) approve of. They hire him and pass the cost on to you along with the 15% agency commission on top of that.

The agency makes 15% on the cost of radio and television spots, too. This cost is most often built into the charge the station quotes as the cost of the air time. If a radio or television station says a 30 second spot at a certain time is going to cost $100, they mean that is what *you* pay. In truth, the agency will charge you $100 and pass along $85 of it to the station, keeping $15 for themselves as their commission.

THE AGENCY-CLIENT RELATIONSHIP

Any professional in the field of advertising will tell you that an agency/client relationship is a very fragile love affair. An agency naturally expects to work very hard in the beginning of the relationship. They have to get to know you and your business and they deliver far more work, usually, than you are paying for. But as time goes on, it becomes easier for the agency to serve your account and that's when they expect to ride the gravy train for a while.

This syndrome is not very different from the experience you may have had with a maid cleaning your home. In the beginning, you tend not to be very demanding, and the maid tends to work very hard to prove herself. As time goes on, you feel her work is slacking off and she feels she is not being paid enough to meet your demands.

Only a very straightforward attitude between the client and the agency can keep the two working together without difficulty. You have a right to demand that the agency does not spend a dime unless you approve of the expenditure in advance. The agency expects you to spend the money you said you were going to spend and that your requests for revisions are kept within limits. You must not approve copy one day and disapprove of it the next. You must not request "little changes" two or three times and then disapprove the entire ad with the comment that you never liked it anyway. No agency of any stature will put up with that sort of behavior very long.

Agency charges are negotiable. Many people believe that an agency always gets 15%. Not always. You are free to negotiate *any* costs with an agency. But the agency is also free to negotiate. There are standards for the industry but there is no law. Actually, some agencies charge 17.65% as a commission rate on all costs.

You might be able to negotiate a 2% discount on *all* billing, particularly if you are paying cash with order and the agency has your retainer in its bank account. There are other costs in need of clear agreement before you "marry" an agency. For instance, an ambitious brochure may cost as much as five thousand dollars to print. You should expect to pay preparation charges, carefully estimated before work starts. You will also pay the printer's cost plus a 15% agency commission. But what about the agency commission on reorders of the brochure? Do you pay 15% commission on those reorders, too? Make sure there is clear agreement on this subject before going ahead.

HOW TO FIND A GOOD ADVERTISING AGENCY

There do exist good smaller agencies who will be happy to take on your small account. This is particularly true in smaller cities. How do you find them?

You can talk to friends who, like you, have a small business. You probably see their advertising and, if you like it, ask them who prepares it. Unless your friend is a competitor of yours, he'll be glad to tell you.

Another way is to check the newspapers, television and radio yourself for advertising you like. Don't pick a national account like Coca-Cola. Find a local advertiser who is doing advertising you think has the look and attitude you want your ads to have. It does not matter if you have a dress shop and he has a television repair store or a car wash. Call him up and ask him who prepares his advertising.

Some of the time, you'll find he does the advertising himself. But if he uses an agency, get the name and the name of the person who handles his account at the agency. Call up. Tell the agency person what business you're in, roughly how much money you intend to spend and ask if they'd be interested in meeting with you to explore the possibility of working together. (The agency should pay for the lunch.)

Often the biggest advantage of using an agency is getting good copy. Many business people really know how to run a business but they cannot write a headline. In fact, the better they are in business, the more they hate the fact that they cannot write advertising. They don't like failure and they don't like inadequacy. They start to write an ad feeling it is going to be terrible. And usually it is.

If you're one of those people, explore the possibility of using an advertising agency. If you find an agency you want to work with, ask them to give you their standard letter of agreement. It is a contract and therefore should be complete. Don't be thrilled if it is short and easy to read. Such a contract probably leaves out too many items that should be covered—items like the ones already mentioned. It should spell out exactly what they are going to charge you for.

Most important: It should spell out what the retainer pays for and what it does not pay for, and under what circumstances it will be returned to you.

Equally important: Since a contract cannot possibly list all of the activity that may go on and who pays for what, *make sure there is a sentence in the contract that says something to this effect:* NO OTHER FEES OR COMMISSIONS WILL BE CHARGED ON ANY SERVICES PROVIDED WHICH ARE NOT MENTIONED IN THIS AGREEMENT. There may be many subjects not covered which the agency will want to charge you for, such as messenger service. Don't laugh. It can add up.

6

The Media as Your Agency

Newspapers, radio and television stations all will help you prepare your message for the public to see and hear. They will do this only if you are going to spend advertising dollars with them, of course. The cost will run anywhere from zero to more than you can afford. Make certain that any costs involved are reviewed clearly with you before you agree to accept the medium's "help" in preparing your advertising. Here's how it usually goes.

NEWSPAPERS

When you deal with a newspaper, you will be talking to the retail advertising department. This local advertising department may have as many as 25 or 50 people whose only job is to get local advertisers to use the newspaper for advertising. The newspaper will assign one of their retail salespeople to your account. Ordinarily, this person will be the only person at the newspaper you will ever talk to. That's convenient. Whether you want to sign a contract, argue about your bill, place another ad, or whatever, you'll only talk to your retail advertising salesperson.

If you can't write your own ad, the salesperson probably will give it a good college try, and some of them are quite good. You will have to guide the writer in what you want to have stressed—price or exclusivity or whatever.

The newspaper also has an art staff, often very talented. Not only will they lay your ad out so that it looks professionally prepared, they will advise you if they feel you have too much copy or the photo you wish to use is not going to reproduce well.

When you have the copy the way you want it (and not before) you are ready for a layout. This is what the art department does—lays the ad out, deciding on the size and style of the type to be used, how many words to each line, etc. Typical layouts look like the ones shown on the next page.

Review the layout carefully, because now is the time to tell the salesman or the art director that you want the headline larger or smaller, the phone number in the center, or whatever.

You will notice in the sample that there are no words on the layout except the headlines. If some part of the type is indicated as "12 pt," ask your newspaper people to show you a sample of 12-pt type, so that you can judge whether it is large enough or not.

Once you have okayed the layout and the copy is ready, your ad will be prepared with type and photo (if any) and you will be given a proof. This is the first time you'll see all the words in print, along with the picture, on a piece of paper. Actually, your ad will look better in the newspaper than it does in proof form. It will look cleaner and the photo, if any, will look clearer. But basically this is what your ad is going to look like in print. Like it? If not, you can still make changes in either the words or copy. Most papers will not charge you for revisions, but they may not do it more than once without a reasonable charge.

Worse: Revisions take time and usually you will want to run in the paper very soon. The cure for any delay is to make sure you like the copy first and then, make sure you like the layout before you go to a proof.

1 Col. ad - Newspaper

2 col. ad - newspaper layout

No matter what, don't take the attitude that "It will be o.k." It won't. Don't run any ad until it looks precisely the way you want it to. If it fails to generate customers once it appears, you don't want to look back and wish you'd made some changes before spending hundreds of dollars to run an ad that is an advertising failure.

What will the newspaper charge you for all this professional help? Usually, nothing as long as you run the prepared ad in their newspaper. In fact, if you'd like copies of the ad to supply other newspapers to run, you probably won't be charged for them as long as you do not ask for an unreasonable number. These copies are called "slicks" or "repro" (for "reproduction") proofs. Most likely, you will not need more than one or two for other newspapers and there will be no charge. If you require as many as a dozen or more, there may be a charge of a few dollars.

A newspaper will almost never provide photography services without charge. Nor will they produce a sketch of your illustration idea without charge. You must supply all such artwork or pay them to do it for you. If you can hustle these services for free, you will be making advertising history!

Be certain to ask the newspaper their opinion of how any photo you are going to use will reproduce. A photo that looks good in your hand may not reproduce well at all. Usually, only photos in black and white will be acceptable. Color photos cannot be used because they often tend to look like mud when printed in black and white. No matter how the photo reproduces, the risk is yours. No newspaper accepts responsibility for photographic quality in reproduction. They'll give you their opinion of how it is going to look but they won't guarantee anything. Of course, when you get your proof of the ad, you'll get a good idea of how the photo or sketch is going to reproduce.

RADIO

Most radio stations will prepare your radio commercial for you at no charge. One of their local announcers will perform the commercial (on tape) and you will have the chance to approve it before it goes on the air.

The same is true if you wish to perform your own commercial, a very popular local advertising technique. Owners of furniture stores, auto dealerships and the like often do their own commercials. The merit of this idea, discussed further in the chapter on radio advertising, is highly debatable. The technique is tempting. The advertiser gets his ego stroked because all his friends tell him they heard him on the radio. Don't be fooled. If you do your own commercial and it fails to deliver customers into your store, it could be your own personal failure.

No matter whether you do the commercial or use one of the station people, there will be no charge unless you wish to use the town's leading disc jockey. In that case, there might be a small "talent fee" charged, only because the disc jockey is very popular.

When the commercial is recorded by you (or someone else), you will be given a tape cassette copy of it for reference. Be careful! Don't give a tape made by one station to another station to run. This material is usually the legal property of the station which made it, and you have no right to use it for anything other than reference.

TELEVISION

With television the story is quite different. In the early days of television, local stations prepared local commercials for advertisers without charge in order to successfully compete with radio. As time went on and costs rose for studio production, television stations began making small charges. Nowadays, most stations charge a substantial fee for producing commercials and some don't do it at all. Union labor controls every person in the studio in any but the smallest markets. You will be dismayed at the cost that will be quoted for any but the simplest television commercial.

An important local advertiser such as the leading furniture store in town may write a contract with a television station guaranteeing that the store will appear on that station 24 or 36 times each week for an entire year. In the case of a fat contract like that, a television station will be tempted to contribute the cost of preparing the commercial. They may split the costs or they may pick up the entire tab. But if you're an occasional advertiser who runs 6 or even 12 spots a week only three or four weeks a year, they can't afford to help you with production on a very grand scale.

What if the station pays all costs for the preparation of your commercial and you decide you wish to run it on the competition station as well as on the station which made the commercial? The producer won't like it, and will charge you a small fee for the "dub" but he will do it. After all, a contract is at stake here and he wants your good will. Whatever you do, don't run it on another station without the written permission of the station that produced it.

7

How Newspaper Advertising Gets Done

If you are going to advertise in a newspaper, one of the smartest things you can do when you first visit with your retail advertising sales representative is to take a tour of the newspaper. This is very easy to arrange and it will teach you "the flow" of newspaper publishing. What gets done where, and when, and how long does it take? You'll probably find it interesting—even if you don't, it is something you should know if you are going to do your own advertising.

"Screening," "Proofing," "Makeup," and "Layout" are words you'll learn in this chapter. It will make you feel secure when you hear these words tossed around when you visit the newspaper. You won't be investing more than an hour of your time and it will be one of the best hours you have ever spent on your advertising education.

THE RATE CARD—THE "PRICE TAG" ON ADVERTISING

Every newspaper in the country publishes a "rate card." It tells exactly what the paper is going to charge you if you run your advertising in it. Actually, a newspaper publishes several rate cards, or one with several sections. The reason for this is that the cost is different to appear in the sports section (perhaps) from the cost to appear in the entertainment section.

The rate card will also tell you if the newspaper is going to charge you for the preparation of your ad, the cost of slicks, etc. If a charge is going to be made for any service, it is usually spelled out in the rate card.

You'll quickly learn to skip over the unwanted material in your local newspaper's rate card to find just the information you need to plan your advertising.

All newspaper rate cards begin with the newspaper name, address and telephone number. They state the days of publication (E is Evening; D is Daily; S is Sunday); the cost to run an ad on each day will vary.

NATIONAL VERSUS LOCAL RATES

You will be buying at the local rate in all cases because the national rate is designed for large national advertisers such as Pepsi Cola. The rates quoted for the national rates include agency commission, but the rates quoted for local advertisers does not. Local rates are always less expensive than national rates. If you use an agency, it will add a commission of 15% to the local rate.

NEGOTIATING NEWSPAPER RATES

Newspaper rates as quoted in their rate cards are almost never negotiable. And if a newspaper does not include agency commissions in its local rates, you will not be able to "negotiate" to get it included. Newspapers go to great lengths to give you every discount imaginable, but you will rarely be successful in negotiating to pay less than the rate card.

HOW NEWSPAPER COSTS ARE FIGURED

When you buy space in the newspaper for your ad, you are charged by the line. One line in one column has a certain

charge depending on which edition you go into. If Sunday
has a bigger circulation than Daily, as is most often the case,
you will pay more for each line you buy in the Sunday
edition.

All lines in all newspapers are the same height—one
agate line. Why do they look different from paper to paper?
Because the newspaper may choose to print its stories more
than one agate line high. They may also put more space
between each line. An example is the *Wall Street Journal*,
which uses larger type and puts more space between each
line of type than do most local newspapers. But when they
sell advertising space they all sell it the same way—by the
agate line.

The professional makes use of a ruler that looks like the
one you used in high school except that instead of being
marked off in inches, it will be marked off in agate lines.
Perhaps, it will be marked off in both inches and agate lines.
It's a good ruler to have in your office and is available in
most art stores. Some newspapers give them away,
complete with an advertising message.

There are fourteen agate lines to the inch, and some
papers do not sell space by the agate line but rather by the
inch. This is a simple exception to deal with. If your
advertisement measures one column in width and 28 agate
lines in height, you are going to pay for twenty-eight agate
lines (or two inches) of space. If your advertisement
measures two columns wide and twenty-eight agate lines in
height, you are going to pay for fifty-six agate lines or four
inches of space. So *agate lines times column width equals
advertisement size.*

Now you can sit at your desk and doodle the
approximate size of an advertisement you'd like to run. You
can measure the ad; once you know the total agate lines, you
multiply that total by the line rate and you know what that
ad size will cost to run once.

FREQUENCY AND SIZE DISCOUNTS

To get you to advertise as much as possible, all newspapers and magazines are on a cheaper-by-the-dozen basis. The more lines you buy, the less each line costs. So, you may find that an ad which will cost you $500 to run once will only cost you $400 each time you run it if you run it six or eight or ten times.

Newspapers keep track of how many lines you use during a year's time. Some (not all!) newspapers will give you a discount at the end of the year if your total lines used warrants it. Others will give you this earned discount only if you have signed a contract.

THE CONTRACT

To lock you in as a customer, the newspaper may ask you if you wish to sign a contract whereby you guarantee to run so many lines in an upcoming year. If you actually run all those lines—if you actually run your ad each week, for example—you will pay substantially less per line for the space. In other words, your bill for that $500 ad will only be $400 because you have promised to run it or some other ad many more times during the coming year.

But what if you don't order all the space you have guaranteed in your contract? That brings us to the old bugaboo, the short rate.

THE SHORT RATE

If you don't run all the ads you promised you would run, the paper is going to ask you to pay the rate applying to the lesser amount of space. Let's say an ad would cost $500 to run once. It might cost $450 each time to run twelve times.

You contracted for twelve times but only ran six. They are going to charge you six times $500. This is the short rate. No, they are not taking you to the cleaners; this is standard industry practice.

But, what if the opposite is true? What if you guarantee to run six times and actually run twelve times during the contract period? Again, the paper will apply the correct rate and give you a nice refund check.

Since it is very difficult to predict your advertising needs a full year in advance, should you sign a maximum-discount contract you may not meet and thereby have to pay a short rate, or should you sign a minimum contract and probably receive a refund?

You can protect your cash flow by paying out as little as possible each week for your advertising, but that short-rate bill always has a way of appearing when you can least afford it, and it must be paid promptly or the paper will shut you off. Not only will they not honor your credit, they may not even accept your advertising for cash in advance.

On the other hand, overpaying each week just to get a refund check at the end of a year's time is money out of your pocket each week which could go to other expenses. The choice is yours.

COMBINATION RATES

When a rate card quotes a line rate or an inch rate, it usually does so in at least three columns—Daily, Evening and Sunday. Then there is a different (and cheaper) line rate for D + E and yet another column for D + E + S. It looks like the example shown on the next page.

As you can see, we get one discount because we run in all editions, and we get another discount based on the number of lines or inches we are running.

INCH RATES FOR SPACE AGREEMENTS
(The space shown must be used each month
for twelve consecutive months)

Column Inches	Daily Only	Eve Only	D+E	Sun Only	D+Sun	D+E+Sun
10	51.20	43.40	75.00	60.00	91.00	125.00
15	46.00	39.25	71.25	57.00	85.00	118.00
20	44.25	38.05	69.90	55.50	83.25	114.70
25	41.70	36.90	67.10	53.90	81.10	110.60

and so on.

RATE HOLDERS

Discounts in the magazine sections of newspapers such as the TV listing pages are usually based on how many times a year you will run your ad. Rateholders can help you take advantage of maximum contract discounts *without* running your ad every week or every month. Here's how they work:

Suppose you have an ad which measures two columns wide by five inches deep—a total of ten inches. Most likely, the best discount will be earned by running your ad each week for 52 weeks. But you don't want to run it 52 weeks in a row. Either you don't need that big an ad each week or you simply cannot afford it. How can you *still* earn the 52-time rate?

Simple: You prepare an ad that is as small as the newspaper will allow you to run. Perhaps it's only one inch, which is one tenth your regular size. This one-inch ad is called a "rateholder," and is run whenever you do not run your big ad. The savings are obvious and substantial.

Even if you run your large ad only ten times and run the rate holder the other forty-two issues of the year, you will get the lower rate for your large ad. If you run the large ad ten times, the savings from getting a fifty-two-times rate will be important to you.

Rate holders are used mostly by advertisers in magazines and not in any other medium, but some newspapers offer them for their television magazine section. If that is where you are going to advertise, look into the possibility of getting more for your dollar.

Perhaps you will want to sign up only for the thirteen-times rate and run your big ad three times and the rate holder ten times. There will still be a substantial saving on the three times you are going to run the big ad.

Check it out thoroughly with the newspaper.

COMBINED (AFFILIATED) NEWSPAPERS

Sometimes a newspaper owns or is affiliated with a newspaper in another city. If you place your advertisement in both of these papers, you will receive yet another discount. It is not uncommon for five or six newspapers to be affiliated in this way. They thus blanket a very large area surrounding your city. These newspaper affiliations are really designed for large advertisers who have stores in several cities in one section of the country and are rarely useful to the small, local advertiser. It may be that it provides you with only "waste" circulation but it may be useful, so check it out.

CLOSING DATES

All newspapers publish their "closing dates" in their rate cards. This is the day (and time, usually) after which no advertising will be accepted. For a Sunday edition, it is often Wednesday or Thursday noon. Don't think you can place a Sunday advertise-ment on Friday afternoon. The paper is printing part of its Sunday issue then and you've lost the chance to advertise your sale.

Usually, closing dates cannot be extended even if the paper wanted to do it, so take your closings seriously.

The closing date and time applies to the reservation of space—the last moment you have to reserve space for your ad in an upcoming issue. Usually, you can provide the paper with the actual ad the next day. Not always. Be sure you don't reserve space and then have no ad to put in the paper. You'll probably have to pay for the space anyway.

POSITION AND PLACEMENT

Where your ad appears in the newspaper is the "position." The back page of any section of any newspaper is considered very valuable placement because that page is exposed to the reader (if only by accident) more frequently than any other pages. But you'll notice that the back page of any section of your local newspaper most often carries a full-page ad. You won't have much luck in getting a small ad on that page.

Paid Position. Most newspapers will honor your request to appear in a certain section such as sports. They will not guarantee placement. Certain other sections such as entertainment (movies, etc.) always cost more because they have a larger readership.

Even if you order a particular section, however, and agree to pay a premium price to get there, the newspaper will not guarantee that you will appear there. The entertainment section is designed for that kind of news, and if there is no room to run your store ad, they'll simply run you in some other section. Some papers have a firm rule that nothing except entertainment ads go on those pages; even if you offer to pay the premium price, they won't accept your advertisement for that section.

If you don't care what section you run in, you order "ROP." This means "run of press" and means the paper will put you where they think it will do you the most good and where they can best accommodate your ad size. Actually, the paper tries to have your best interest at heart because the success of your ad in their paper means more advertising by you in their pages.

Right-Hand Page. Appearing on the right-hand page is considered more valuable than appearing on the left-hand page because it is the first page we see when we turn a page. Is it really more valuable? No one knows, although a lot of money has been spent on research projects to establish the fact. Research say it's better. Is it? Who knows?

Gutter. Unfold your newspaper so you are looking at two pages at once. The center—where the two pages meet—is called the "gutter." It's easy to understand that ad placement in a column next to the gutter is not as eye-catching as placement in an outside column.

Can you avoid appearing next to the gutter? You can request "right-hand page, outside column" and it won't cost you an extra dime—but there will be no guarantee that you will be given that placement. Almost no newspaper will give you that promise. So you put your money down and you trust to luck. Of course, the better friend you are of the sales rep and the more influence he or she has in the press room, the better chance you have of avoiding the gutter.

The fact is, if you have a good-looking ad, people are going to see it. If it is easy to read and provocative, they will read it. And if it contains an offer they cannot refuse, they will appear magically in your store to buy.

Some newspapers are inconsiderate enough to run your ad right next to a competitor's! There is nothing you can do about this except plead with the newspaper for better separation. If you think it won't hurt because your ad looks so much better, don't bet on it. Not everyone may agree that your ad (or offer) is more appealing.

PRINTING IN REVERSE

Newspaper and magazine ads are normally printed with black ink on white paper. A publisher can "reverse" the process so it looks as though it were done with white ink on black paper. A big blob of black on a page with white letters in it seems to stand out from the rest of the page, and is very tempting to use when you're doing everything you can to call the reader's attention to your ad.

Reverse printing is used often—but it is not a good idea. If it doesn't work, why do so many people use it? It is impossible to pick up a newspaper or magazine and not find a reverse ad. Is everyone that stupid? Maybe not, but there are more than a few advertisers who use reverse incorrectly. How do you do it right for maximum effectiveness?

To start with, do a little research of your own. Clip out half a dozen reverse ads from your local newspaper. Put them on the desk in front of you and stare at them. Here's what you'll see:

1.   A reverse ad cannot carry a photograph. If it does, the photo seems to not be part of the ad because all the rest of the ad is on a black background.

2.   The type in a reverse ad should be large. Small type in reverse tends to be very difficult to read. Your prospective customer will notice your ad, but will not work hard to read it. So use larger and fewer words in a reverse ad.

3.   If there is another reverse ad on the page or on the page facing yours, it will compete with your ad for attention. If it is larger than your ad, it will win the battle for attention and your ad won't be given the readership you hope for by using reverse.

There is another danger involved in using reverse type. High-speed presses when printing in revers can easily "lay down" too much ink, which makes letters like "o" and "a" fill in and merely become blots on the page.

There is no arguing the fact that ads in reverse tend to stand out on the page. If they are prepared properly, they can improve readership. Just make certain when you see your proof that you can read your ad easily and the type is not blurred.

SCREENING

Screening is something all newspapers and magazines do in order to print a photograph. It is also used to keep too much black ink from being laid down on a page and showing through on the other side. If you have an ad prepared in reverse and want to see a big, black ad with white type—don't be surprised when the black comes out gray!

LEADING

"Leading" rhymes with "heading" and refers to the amount of space between each line of type in an advertisement. Leading takes up space, of course, and limits the amount of copy you can use in a given area, but it makes your ad easier to read. The lines of type will not be so close together that they resemble an insurance policy. Spend a little more money to "lead out" your copy and make it more attractive to your reader.

Look at the space ad shown on the next page in two versions—one with and one without extra leading. Which one would you prefer to read?

BORDERS

Borders outline your ad and unless your ad is very large, borders are valuable in separating it from adjoining material in the newspaper. Always try to use a border.

MODELING
IT'S A MAN'S JOB!
At Barbizon men train for modeling or personal grooming by appearing before TV cameras, posing for photographers, performing in fashion shows. For 32-page book, without obligation, mail ad or CALL
XXX-YYY-ZZZZ
The Barbizon School
Dept. XXX address, city, zip
name age
address zip
city phone ( )
(area code)

MODELING
IT'S A MAN'S JOB!
At Barbizon men train for modeling or personal grooming by appearing before TV cameras, posing for photographers, performing in fashion shows. For 32-page book, without obligation, mail ad or CALL
XXX-YYY-ZZZZ
The Barbizon School
Dept. XXX address, city, zip
name age
address zip
city phone ( )
(area code)

Borders can also make your ad more eye-catching. They add little to the cost and it's hard to think of a case where they won't help the readership of your ad.

Look at the two ads on the next page. They are the same ad, but one has a border around it. The other, with identical copy and photo, has not had this treatment. Notice how the border helps contain the message as well as separate it from other material which will be right alongside it in the newspaper.

WHITE SPACE

Any portion of your advertisement that does not have type on it is "white space." You pay the newspaper as much for white space as you do for type, and in your effort to take up no more space than necessary while saying a lot, you may sacrifice this white space. That's what makes an ad look like a page in a telephone directory—all crowded together and too difficult to read.

You simply cannot eat your cake and have it, too. Try to resist the natural temptation to fill the entire space of your ad with your message. White space offers the reader a little relief from the crowded messages in the ads surrounding yours, and will draw his eye to your ad even though he won't know it's happening. And that is what you want.

NEWSPAPER INSERTS

Here's a way to advertise in a newspaper and spend less money than you would spend for advertising in that newspaper! Sound good? Sure. But there are drawbacks. You prepare and print inserts. The newspaper will tell you how many to print. It will be a little more than their total circulation, probably, unless you are buying only part of their circulation, perhaps in only one area.

BARBIZON

because looking good is our business

You can BE A MODEL or...just look like one. We teach men and women Professional Modeling for the poise and confidence needed in today's competitive world.

Find out how Professional Modeling training can give you "the look" that helps any career. Classes forming now, so get our free 32-page illustrated book, without obligation, to all 13 and older. Mail coupon **TODAY** or **PHONE 296-6366.**

BARBIZON SCHOOL 296-6366
452 Fashion Valley E., S.D., 92108
name_____ age_____
address_____ zip_____
city_____ phone_____

BARBIZON

because looking good is our business

You can BE A MODEL or...just look like one. We teach men and women Professional Modeling for the poise and confidence needed in today's competitive world.

Find out how Professional Modeling training can give you "the look" that helps any career. Classes forming now, so get our free 32-page illustrated book, without obligation, to all 13 and older. Mail coupon **TODAY** or **PHONE 296-6366.**

BARBIZON SCHOOL 296-6366
452 Fashion Valley E., S.D., 92108
name_____ age_____
address_____ zip_____
city_____ phone_____

Review these options with your newspaper representative and do not buy more circulation than you need.

The newspaper will have some rules about size and paper weight. You can't print on cardboard, for example, and you can't print on a huge piece of unfolded paper, but that's about where the rules end.

You can print on any color paper. You can use as many colors as you wish. You have almost total freedom to prepare anything you like.

You prepare the insert and have it delivered to the newspaper. They insert it in the issue of the paper you want to go in, and they distribute your insert along with their newspaper to their readers.

The benefits sound wonderful: Your message will be alone on a page, not surrounded by other advertising, and your message will cost less than it would if you were to buy the same size space in the newspaper itself.

Now for the drawbacks: Newspaper inserts must be prepared far in advance of publication date, in most cases. If you contract with a newspaper to run an insert, and for any reason you don't do it, there is usually a penalty, and it could be a large part of the total you were going to spend. Be sure you know the terms and that you have read the contract carefully before you sign it.

Another disadvantage is potential readership. The paper may have a huge circulation (for which you must print a huge number of inserts) but how many will read your insert? Many people throw away ad inserts that come in the newspaper, and as a matter of habit read only the newspaper itself.

Don't think that because a newspaper has a circulation of 100,000, your message will reach that many people. Sixty percent is a good achievement.

COST OF INSERTS

The cost of inserts varies all over the lot. First of all is the cost of printing the insert itself. How ambitious can you afford to be? Can you afford to print a large number of inserts in full color? Most likely there will be other inserts in the issue you're using, and if they are in full color and you are in black and white, your readership will suffer.

The cost of a newspaper insert will vary from paper to paper and market to market. It will cost more to insert in your city's leading newspaper than it will in one issue of your neighborhood PENNYSAVER. So call the newspaper representatives and check the costs and terms of inserts, and compare those costs between the leading newspaper and the least expensive newspaper in your market.

As a local business, you will most likely be in better shape by going with the local PENNYSAVER or its equivalent. The leading newspaper might provide far too much waste circulation to make inserts worthwhile to you.

COMPETITIVE INSERTS

About the worst thing that can happen to you is to prepare an insert and then find that, in the same paper, there is an insert produced by your competition!

The competition may even be making a better offer to the reader than your offer. What a disappointment! Avoid it by asking the newspaper for *competitive protection*. They may not grant it, but surely they will tell you if your competition plans to run an insert with the same issue. If they do, ask for contractual permission to delay your insert—and delay it long enough to give you time to re-write your ad to make a better offer to the consumer.

THE UNDENIABLE BENEFITS OF INSERTS

Even considering the negatives involved with inserts, you should not be turned away from their potential. There is great value to delivering your message on your own piece of paper where it will look impressive and not have to compete with the rest of the newspaper page for reader attention. This value is increased if you use a discount coupon in your message or if you want to itemize products or services on sale.

Another benefit of inserts is that you may wish to print enough copies to insert in three or four issues of the newspaper over a period of weeks or months. This reduces printing costs as well as newspaper charges, and should be considered in your planning.

8

All About Radio and Television Advertising

You don't have to be a professional advertising person for twenty years to know that radio is different from television. Most of that difference, however, is in the creative work: what you say and how you say it. The *business* of radio and television is very similar. For that reason, they are discussed together in this chapter. Where there is a difference between the two in how you do business, it is reviewed it in detail.

RADIO AND TELEVISION RATE CARDS

They look remarkably alike because both radio and television sell commercial time the same way—in segments of one minute. They will sell you ten seconds or twenty or thirty or forty-five or sixty seconds. Some stations offer fifteen seconds as well. Most commercials are thirty seconds long on both radio and television. Hardly anyone uses 60s or 120s on television any more except used car dealers and even they mostly buy 30s.

As with newspaper rates, radio and television time is "cheaper by the dozen." There's one rate for a thirty-second commercial if you run it once; a cheaper rate if you run it six times and a far cheaper rate if you run it twelve or twenty-four times in one week.

The radio or television station will offer you a contract just like the newspaper did if you guarantee to run a certain frequency within a certain period of time. They, too, employ the policy of charging a short rate if you do not meet your contract promises. But be careful! Your radio or television contract will probably require you to give them two weeks notice if you wish to cancel your schedule or even adjust it. While the newspaper will not require more than a couple of days to either put your ad in the paper or cancel it that one week, the radio or television station usually has the right to require two week's notice to change your schedule.

"WHEEL AND DEAL" ON RADIO AND TELEVISION

All radio and television rates are highly negotiable! This even includes the $500,000 charged for thirty seconds on the Super Bowl football game. Although all radio and television stations have rate cards, those rates can be pared down, depending on how much you're going to advertise, and how much unsold time is available when you want to go on air.

PREEMPTABLE RATES

One of the things a radio or television station will do in order to make as much money as possible is offer you a low rate on the understanding that if some other advertiser comes along before air time and will pay them the rate quoted on the rate card, you will not go on the air as promised. The advertising time will be given to the highest bidder.

This is known as the "preempt" rate and it is customary. For a highly popular time period, however, many stations will not even offer a preempt rate because they are sold out at the rate card price and there is no chance you will go on the air.

Always buy the preemptable rate if they will give it to you. They would not offer it if there weren't a good chance you will actually go on the air. Further, some smart sales managers in radio and television will give you a preempt rate in a popular time slot at least a couple of times just to prove to you that their station will be rewarding for you. Once they've proven that, they will charge you the full rate by refusing preemptable rates at that time period.

REPEAT—"WHEEL AND DEAL"

Whether you are talking rate card or talking preemptable rates, always wheel and deal. If the rate card says that a spot is going to cost $50, offer them $200 for five spots instead of four. They may choose to identify the fifth spot as a "bonus" so they can always say they didn't go below rate card for the sale, but the fact is that you got each spot for $40, not $50.

COMPETITIVE ADVERTISING

This is a tough one. If your competition is *not* advertising on the station, it will be a sales tool for the station to be able to tell your competitors that you *are* advertising on the station. That's worth something and should help you wheel and deal. On the other hand, if your competition *is* advertising on that station, you must be certain to ask for contract verification that the station will not put your competitor's advertising on the air within thirty minutes of your commercial. (More than that, you will not get!)

CLOSINGS

All radio and television stations have closing times just as newspapers have. We've already discussed the fact that you may need two weeks to cancel or adjust your time purchases, but if you have a new commercial you want to put on the air, you cannot do it the same day. It will always take two or three days to feed the new commercial into the computer. Don't miss the opportunity to run your on-sale

by failing to deliver the commercial to the radio or
television station in time for them to use it.

AGENCY COMMISSION

All radio and television rates include agency commission,
and the rate card should tell you that clearly. If you do not
have an agency, you can earn the agency commission simply
by telling the station that the John Smith Advertising
Agency is the agency for John Smith's Furniture Store. Most
radio and television stations will "recognize" you as an
agency if you ask them to. But you must ask, or you will be
billed non-commissionable. Fight for this. It is 15% of your
total bill and can represent a lot of money over a year.

RATINGS

Volumes have been written on the development and
validity of rating systems. The fact is that no one has ever
really proven them to be valid. No one has ever proven
them to be invalid, either. They exist, and radio and
television stations pay a fortune for the information that is
provided by them.

All stations would like to be the leaders in "the ratings."
If a station salesman tells you the station leads in the 5-7
p.m. time period, ask to see his book. Make him prove it.
Rating books take a good bit of education to read and
interpret correctly, but a station salesman should be able to
illustrate his point of superiority to you and convincingly
illustrate it or he's a rotten salesman.

There are a few "buzz words" you might wish to know
because they get tossed around like a salad. Here are the
common ratings expressions:

Rating. A "ten" rating means that 10% of all the radio or
television sets in the area were turned on and tuned in to

that station. If we know how many sets exist in the area (and we do), we can quickly calculate how many sets were tuned in to this station at a particular time. But there is more we need to know, as you'll see below.

Share. A "twenty-five share" means that, of the sets that were turned on at a particular time, 25% were tuned to that station. Of course, if you're talking about 3 a.m., there probably weren't many television sets turned on and a twenty-five share doesn't mean very much.

But at least, with the rating and share, we have two good indicators of which station is really getting attention at a particular time. Now we need to know something else.

Audience. A station with a ten rating and a twenty-five share might look very good, but if the time period you are talking about was Saturday morning, the bulk of the audience was probably children under twelve. Is that who you want looking at your television commercial? Likewise, those same figures applied to a 6 p.m. newscast leads us to guess that almost no children or teenagers were watching. Audience composition figures in the ratings book will tell us who was watching.

There are many other figures provided by the ratings book, such as HUT figures (the total number of "homes using television" at a particular time) and SIU figures ("sets in use" for radio). If you want to take the complete course, talk to your radio or television time salesman. All you really need to know is rating, share, and audience composition.

If the salesman starts throwing around other statistics, such as cumulative audience, forget it. The "cume" is how many homes they reach in total over a day's or a week's time. If you're only going to be on the air once a day for three days a week, what do you care about the "cume?"

STATION X VERSUS STATION Y

Most markets have a gaggle of radio stations and at least four television stations—three network stations and at least one independent station. If there are not four in your city, there are four in the big town down the road and you'll be using at least one of them.

Let's concentrate on television for a moment, for here's a case where radio differs from television: Use all television stations, if you can. Resist the temptation to concentrate your advertising on any one station simply because they are the cheapest or the salesman is easier to deal with.

All television stations have a hard core of loyal viewers (as do radio stations). If you omit that station from your advertising efforts, you are ignoring the potential for getting your message across to the largest possible audience.

As a small advertiser, you won't be able to go on all four stations at the same time—or even the same week—but you can use all stations over a period of time, and even the station that is the weakest in its ability to deliver customers will provide you with some customers you won't reach any other way.

On radio, the situation is different because radio stations tend to program to certain audiences. There will be a station for classical music which appeals to the more affluent, educated portion of the population (they say that, anyway) and there will be a leading rock music station which claims to "own" the teenage audience, etc.

The audience composition figures in the ratings books will be your first clue as to which radio station to use, but for television, try to use all stations over a period of time.

CABLE TELEVISION

"Cable penetration"—the number of homes or the percentage of homes in an area with cable television—is growing so fast that even to quote a figure in this book would be useless. The percentage varies greatly from market to market, but you should consider and investigate it in your market. Find out how they're doing by calling them and asking for a salesman to visit you to tell you his story.

This is particularly true if you want to reach a certain segment of the population. For example, MTV is an excellent vehicle for teenagers and young adults. CNN is a leader with older, more affluent and retired persons. Get the story before you dismiss it as something that is not for your advertising.

OUT-OF-HOME LISTENING

More than fifty percent of all radio listening is done out of the home—at the beach or in the backyard or in the automobile. This is a huge audience, and for obvious reasons can only be estimated. Don't overlook it, because it is not included in the ratings figures.

DO YOUR OWN RESEARCH

One of the most profitable things you can do in planning your own advertising is to ask your customers what radio and television stations they tune into and when.

Develop a postcard-size form and ask them to fill it out. People usually love to take part in "surveys." If you find out that 70% of your customers listen to a certain radio station, you really must give that station a chance to carry your message.

It's a simple bit of research and it has great validity. If not one of your customers listens to the leading radio station in your city, you had better think twice about going on that station, no matter what their rating or share or composition.

CREATING RADIO AND TELEVISION COMMERCIALS

Your radio or television commercial should be created by someone who has both the talent and the training to provide you with a commercial which will impress the audience. The commercial only lasts for thirty seconds; in that brief time, you have to get on, make your offer and get off. Most important, you have to stand out and be impressive when you are surrounded by other messages which were prepared by professionals. The thirty seconds fly by so fast that only a professional can make each second work for you.

THE SOURCES FOR CREATIVE MATERIAL

If you work with an advertising agency, they will prepare your radio or television commercials. They will write it and review it with you for your approval before producing it. The problem you may have to deal with is this: What if you don't like the commercial they have prepared? If you have a solid reason for not liking the commercial, they will most likely re-write it. But most often, you simply do not feel it is impressive. You are made to feel that you must accept their work almost on blind faith. That is one of the great drawbacks in working with an agency when you are a small account. You may feel you are being "steam-rollered" into using material you have little faith in.

WRITE THE COMMERCIAL YOURSELF

Very dangerous. Just as you may have said, "I can write a better ad than that," it is very easy to sit at home in front of the television set and say, "I can write my own commercial and it will be better than my competition's." Perhaps it will. But you must be very honest in your appraisal of your creative work, and that is hard to do. There is a great temptation to tell the public what you want them to know instead of telling them what they want to hear about.

If you want one, single rule about producing advertising messages, it would be, "Make them an offer they can't refuse." If you have not done this, you will fail.

FREELANCE WRITERS AND PRODUCERS

This is, perhaps, your best source of creative material. It's hard to find good freelance people because they don't have offices with signs on the front of them. They're not in the yellow pages.

You may find them through other business friends who use freelance people. As previously mentioned, you can look at local television commercials and listen to the radio. When you come across a commercial you think does a good job, call up the sponsor and ask him who prepared the material.

The radio or television station or television production house may steer you to good freelance people. They may even have good people on their staff.

Staff writers are good because if you don't like what they have written, they will re-write it without a lot of fuss. After all, if you don't like the radio commercial that a radio station has prepared, you won't go on the air and they won't make any money from you.

So the first source you should investigate for your creative material—newspaper or radio or television—is from the advertising medium you intend to use. No matter who you use, there are certain safeguards you can employ which will help you be successful. Her are a few of them:

ARE YOU AN ACTOR?

There has been a growing trend over the years for owners of small businesses to perform their own radio and/or television commercials. The concept has merit. The audience gets a "promise" directly from the owner. When an owner announces that he has the lowest prices in town, the audience may tend to believe it more than they would believe an announcer.

On television, the owner saves the cost of paying the announcer and if the local television performers are any good, they are expensive enough to make you want to save the money. On the other hand, radio announcers at the station you are going to use often charge nothing and they have an audience loyalty that gives them credibility.

It is difficult not to conclude that the reason so many owners do their own commercials is ego. They become stars. People recognize them in restaurants and bars, which makes them think their advertising is working. Unless the owner is a real clod (and, sometimes, even if he is) his performance in a commercial will deliver customers. This is particularly true if the message is well-written. What you don't know is: How much more business you would have done if the commercial had featured a good, professional actor or announcer instead of you?

The leading furniture store retailer in a large market has been performing his own commercials for years. He is fairly young and attractive and speaks well.   Then he did something really smart. He continued to perform in some of his commercials but had a professional announcer for others. The result was an increase in sales while spending the same advertising dollars. That may not turn out to be true in your case at all. The only way you will ever know is to test the concept. Have the same radio commercial (and, television, too) performed by you and a professional actor/announcer. Then air a few commercials using both of you. Who did the best for sales? You or the announcer? Or was it a combination of both? You'll find out fast.

HUMOR IN COMMERCIALS

Watch it! It's very dangerous! First of all, not everyone laughs at the same joke. Second, humor tends to decrease the seriousness of your message.

There's an even worse danger. How many times have you seen or heard a really funny commercial and remember the humor but can't remember the product? Everyone has had that experience. You are not in the entertainment business. You are trying to advertise. Tell the jokes to your customer once he's in your store, but keep the attempt at humor out of your advertising.

TESTIMONIAL ADVERTISING

The concept of having a satisfied customer deliver your message about how terrific you are is a very good one. Expensive research testing by some of the world's largest advertisers has proven time and again that this technique rarely misses. The guidelines are simple. Find a satisfied customer who can talk reasonably well and is believable as the type of person who might shop at your business. Don't use a society matron to sell a plumbing store. Using a glamorous model to sell roofing is dumb. Even if she really is a satisfied customer, no one will believe it.

Another safeguard: The "customer" in your commercial can be an actor and not a real customer at all. There is no law against that. But, he or she must not be "slick." If you have an actor portray a customer, make sure the actor is a little rough around the edges in appearance and performance. It will give reality to the commercial.

But, most of all, remember that the "customer" must be someone the audience can relate to.

DUMB HEROINES

The advertising profession, when describing a television commercial, refers to the customer in the commercial as "our heroine." There are a great many commercials on the air today in which the "heroine" acts stupid. It is most often done with men, for some reason. But the technique provides a "spokesman" for the advertiser who is a goof that no one in the audience wants to relate to. The audience may laugh at and enjoy him, but no sale.

You will probably never see a Proctor and Gamble commercial using that concept. The biggest advertiser in the world knows well that "our hero" must be a hero. The goof can use the competition's product. Our hero buys our product. He is not dumb.

MUSIC IN COMMERCIALS

Music is very valuable in commercials because it does two things at once. It softens the message, making it more appealing to listen to. It provides a "mood" and dramatically highlights your message in a way that a single voice alone cannot achieve.

The most ambitious music for a commercial is the "jingle." The music is specially written for the advertiser and performed by professionals. It is very expensive to produce, even if you use the orchestra from the local Elks Club. Most jingles you see and hear on radio and television are priced out of your league. Fifty thousand dollars is not a lot of money to spend on one, and some original music costs much more. Pepsi Cola might hold the record of expense with its more than one million dollars for Michael Jackson's commercial. Coca-Cola spends more money than you will ever see on just one musical production.

But music is still available for your advertising. It is called "stock music," and every radio and television station has a library of it available for your use at very low cost (maybe $100). Often it is free. Use music whenever you can. It's a chore to listen to dozens of recordings the station has on hand in order to find what you think is the right music for your message, but it's worth the effort.

USING ANIMATION (CARTOONS)

Animation is tricky and expensive. If you consider using animation, you must be in a position to do it as well as Walt Disney Studios do, because that's who the audience will subconsciously compare you with. Good animation costs several hundred dollars per second, which probably puts it out of your budget.

Just in case you find a way to do it within your budget, here's what's tricky about it. Animation works best when it illustrates something that living actors cannot illustrate, such as "living" soap suds, or talking dogs, or Snow White and the Seven Dwarfs. Even then, it isn't always the best way to go. The Judy Garland version of THE WIZARD OF OZ contains no animation, even though it would have been easy to animate The Straw Man or The Cowardly Lion. The fact that the people were real touched our hearts far more than animation ever could have.

COMPUTERIZED PRODUCTION

Computerized techniques are used in more than half of all the commercials you watch in an average evening. Words and people fly through the air, boxes of cereal fly open and empty into cereal bowls and real automobiles zoom along real highways—two feet off the ground! A great deal of this movie magic has been available for years but only by using very expensive techniques of production. Computers have lowered the cost of movie magic tremendously.

The production company that manufactures your television commercial should have these computer techniques available at a price you can afford and should be able to guide you as to how to apply them to your commercial.

"THE FOURTH QUARTER" ON RADIO AND TELEVISION

We've saved the worst for last. Beginning in late September and lasting through December 24 (the fourth quarter), radio and television time sales increase daily. Christmas advertising starts to build and by mid-October it is very difficult to buy television time. The crush may be somewhat lighter on radio, but television always gets to a point where not only is there no "preempt" inventory, there is no inventory at all. Stations are sold out.

You won't find newspapers sold out—they can always print another page of advertising and be thrilled to do it. The problem with newspapers in the fourth quarter is that they are so full of advertising, your small space ad is not going to be noticed by very many people.

It's a particularly tough time for the small advertiser, and often the best thing you can do is to know it's coming and try to live through it. This is particularly true if you are a service business like a beauty parlor or a health spa. If you are a retailer, your problem will be to do an ad large enough to be seen and noticed or to buy radio and television time inexpensively.

9

Direct Response
Advertising

Direct response advertising is advertising which requests direct telephone or written response from the prospective customer. It can take the form of a newspaper ad with a coupon the reader is asked to mail in or a phone number to call in order to receive either information or the product. It can be a radio or television commercial such as the ones which sell phonograph albums "not available at record stores!" You can get them only through direct response.

One of the great advantages of direct-response advertising is that you get an immediate indication of whether or not your offer is any good. It doesn't matter whether you are offering a revolutionary can opener, or a free book on how to become a nurse's aide. You will receive 80% of your total response in the first two or three days after you place a direct response ad or go on a radio or television station with a direct response offer. The final 20% will dribble in over the next weeks and months and even years.

We will discuss direct response advertising by mail in the next chapter. At this point, let's be aware of what you should include in a direct response offer in a newspaper or on radio or television. On the next page is a sample of a direct response newspaper ad.

Notice these important features:

1. The coupon is surrounded by a border of dashes or dots—something to outline the coupon. This signals the customer to clip the ad out of the newspaper. This border is very important. It demands reader action.

2. There is sufficient room for the reader to fill out the coupon. Probably you yourself have tried to fill out coupons without enough room to write.

3. The coupon used in our illustration gives the advertiser's name, address and phone number even though the same information may appear elsewhere in the ad. This is very important. Many people clip out the coupon and save it—not the whole ad. The next day, they may not know where to mail the coupon unless the name and address of the store is on the coupon.

BUILD YOUR MAILING LIST

Save the coupons you receive. They are going to become your permanent mailing list. Type the information neatly on cards or sheets of paper, if you wish, so you don't wind up with a big box of yellowing coupons. But save the information. You may wish to advertise to them again one day. You also may be able to sell your list to other advertisers or to a mailing-list house.

DIRECT RESPONSE ADDS TO YOUR COSTS

By including a reasonable-sized coupon in your ad, thus making it a direct-response ad, you are adding substantially to the cost of the ad. So don't do a direct response ad without a good reason. But if you can develop an offer that makes it worth the time and postage of the reader to clip the coupon and fill it out and mail it back to you, you're halfway home to gaining a new customer.

DIRECT RESPONSE ON RADIO AND TELEVISION

Can you do a good direct-response commercial in 30 seconds? You bet you can! For years, the big boys felt that direct response on radio and television needed two minutes to do the job right. It took these advertising geniuses years to learn that, just as in print, make your offer and then shut up is the way consumers like it.

There is one real problem with direct response on radio or television—no coupon, only a telephone number. The big boys tell us that the way to combat this problem is to give the phone number four times! There are those of us who feel that shouting a phone number four times only turns off an audience. So what do you do?

Give the phone number once or even twice if you like, but always add the words: "Look us up in the white pages."

Why the white pages? Why not the yellow pages? Because if the prospect turns to the yellow pages and likes your competitors' ads better than she likes yours, you've lost. Don't take chances.

When we talk about advertising in the yellow pages later in this book, you'll find that we're enthusiastic about them as an advertising tool. But the truth is that there is one big drawback: They display your competitor's ads right alongside yours, and there is no way to get around that.

DISCOUNT COUPONS

Including a discount coupon in your newspaper ad is not really a form of direct-response advertising. An offer of $1.00 off purchase price might well bring customers into your store, but you don't need an expensive coupon in your ad to do that. One line of copy will achieve the same result. Just say, "$1.00 off by presenting this ad at time of purchase."

Lastly, if you put a discount offer in your ad, include an expiration date. Otherwise, people will present the ad for discount a hundred years from today!

10

Direct Mail Advertising

Direct mail can be the most expensive, complicated and sophisticated way to advertise there is. Volumes have been written on how to do it right. It is such a special form of advertising that there are agencies which do nothing else. Some of them are very large and expensive.

Your local yellow pages will list direct mail agencies, and you may wish to confer with one or two. However, your best source for a recommendation is a friend with a small business who works with a direct mail agency and likes what is being done.

If you pick an agency out of the telephone directory, make sure you *start* by getting references—other businesses like yours they have worked for. Talk with these people to get a clear indication of the professional ability of the agency, how they do business, their charges, and if their interest in a small account is genuine.

Direct mail is an ideal tool for the small business to use in building sales. It can be inexpensive, simple and effective. And you can do it yourself.

If you decide to produce a direct mail piece yourself, you must be careful to control costs by thorough planning, because costs can get out of hand at every step along the way. Just the cost of postage for a one-time mailing is a big expense. You could buy more than few newspaper ads for the money the postage will cost!

HOW DIRECT MAIL WORKS

Direct mail is used to produce either **sales** or **leads**—to get people to order your service or merchandise or to call or write you for information. So direct mail always says either "Order Now" or "Call Now" or "Return the card now for full information without obligation."

To use direct mail, you are going to spend money on the following items:

1. Return mail (and perhaps bulk mail) permits.
2. The writing, design and production of a mailing piece.
3. The printing of the piece.
4. A list of prospects to mail to.
5. Postage and perhaps envelopes and reply cards.
6. Getting the pieces into the mail.

WHERE DO YOU START?

In using direct mail, you should first decide who to mail to. How do you get their names and addresses? You can get potential customer names from a mailing list house or broker. These are companies in the business of selling a wide variety of lists of names and addresses of people likely to be interested in a particular product or service. Choosing the right list is important to you, to avoid wasting an expensive mailing on people who are not likely to become your customers.

When you advertise your local hardware store in your city's leading newspaper, your ad is going to be seen and read by many people who have a dozen hardware stores closer to their homes than your store. Advertising to these people is called "waste circulation," but it cannot be avoided by a newspaper. Avoiding waste circulation in direct mail is done by selecting the right lists.

The cheapest list you can buy is a zip code list. It will give you the names and addresses of everyone in your zip code area. If you want to reach everyone in your neighborhood, you can buy several zip codes surrounding your store. How many you buy is your choice. You know best how far people will travel to get to your store.

You might wish to buy only doctors in a zip code, or teenage girls, or people older than 50, or people who make over $35,000 per year. You can do this, but the catch is that the more select a list, the more it costs. A zip code list might cost as little as $20 per thousand names. A select list in the same zip codes could cost up to $75 per thousand.

You can find mailing list brokers or houses in your local yellow pages. If they don't have any, try the yellow pages for the nearest large city. Call at least two or three to get competitive prices. All you need to tell them is what kind of list you want to buy (zip code, or all teachers, or dentists, or whatever), and they will tell you how many names they can deliver and how much it will cost per thousand. If the firm you call does not have the list you want, they will usually refer you to someone who does.

You will not be able to buy only a few hundred names. If you want to mail to a list that small, you will have to compile it yourself, from the phone directory or yellow pages.

Commercial lists are sold in multiples of 1,000. If you want only part of a list that has more names on it than you need or can afford, ask for a sampling, done by selecting names from it on a random basis (every fifth or twentieth name, for instance.)

You will have to pay for a list up front; the house will not deliver the list until they get your check. You will also be asked to agree that only you will use the list, and only as many times as the company allows (usually once). If you want to mail to the list again, you must pay the fee again.

The list will be available in your choice of several formats, most of which are for big-time mailers. Your choice should be pressure-sensitive labels, which can be peeled off and stuck onto the mailing pieces or envelopes.

YOUR DIRECT MAIL BUDGET

Once you know how many names you can get and what the list will cost, you can begin preparing a budget. *Do not proceed without a budget!* You don't want to run out of money when the job is half done. Prepare your budget in writing, listing the following items and their costs. For this example, assume you are willing to spend $1 for each piece and that you have bought a list of 5,000 names.

DIRECT MAIL BUDGET

Mailing list of 5,000 names @ $22 per 1,000	$ 110
Prepare and print 5,000 pieces @ $1 each	5,000
Return mail permit fee	160
Bulk mail permit fee	50
Return postage deposit	50
Postage @ 25¢ (first class) for 5,000 pieces	1,250
TOTAL	$6,620

Too expensive! Can't afford it! Ok. But we had to start somewhere. Let's look at those costs.

The mailing list: you could buy just 2,500 names, for $55. Postage will then drop by half as well, to $625. If you do the mailing using bulk-mailing procedures, it will cost even less.

The cost of the mailing piece, anywhere from 50¢ to $3 each, depends on how many you print and how elaborate it is: whether it has a photo, graphics, is printed in more than one color of ink. You've doubtless received fancy, four-color mailing pieces and thrown them away without even looking at them. From now on, you'll feel guilty about that.

A postcard could be the least expensive type of mailing piece, costing only a few cents. It's difficult for a postcard to compete with larger communications in full color, but for some businesses, like gas stations, dry cleaners, repair shops and the like, postcards are perfectly usable and successful.

You can see that preparing a direct mail campaign involves controlling expenses every step along the way. Plan your expenses so that you can do the most attractive and eye-catching mailing piece possible at a cost you can afford.

Even if your budget only allows a postcard mailing, there are things you can do to dress it up, such as

USING COLOR

Preparing a mailing piece in two colors of ink, such as black and red, costs more than one color. Not more than twice, but more. If you use one color of ink, it will cost very little more to use a color other than black. And if you print a color of ink on another color of paper stock (other than white), you can create a colorful piece without the cost.

This is a good trick that can save a lot of money because the printer won't charge much more, if anything, for one color of ink and a color paper stock.

If your piece includes a photo, remember that it will print in the same color as the words, so you might want to use black. You would not want a picture of your product to be in pink or purple!

One more word on the use of color inks. The difference in cost between one color and two is not great—perhaps 15% more. But printing in three or more colors of ink is a whole different story. The price skyrockets because the printing is done on a four-color press, a totally different and much more expensive kind. Also, four-color printing is a specialty: printers who do one- and two-color work usually are not equipped to do three or more colors.

PAPER WEIGHT

Here's a trap you must avoid because it can cost you a lot of money. Sometimes a printer is able to provide a heavier weight of paper which will make your mailing piece look and feel a lot more substantial. He may have it left over from another job, or he has bought a "remnant" or closeout from a paper mill, and he can pass along the savings to you.

Watch out! If using the heavier paper makes your mailing piece (even a postcard) weigh more than one ounce, it will nearly *double* the postage cost. Not much of a "saving," is it?

The opposite is also true. Do not use a paper that is so flimsy that the post office will not accept it. Be sure to call them ahead of time to find out the minimum weight they permit for large mailings. Check also on permissible sizes, if you plan on using a size other than standard.

FOLDED MAILING PIECES

If you take a piece of letter-sized paper and fold it in half, you are looking at four pages, counting front and back. If you fold it in thirds, you will be looking at six pages. Folding gives you a chance to separate your various messages, illustrations or coupons. An illustration of two folded pieces is shown on the next page.

The printer will do the folding for you better than you or someone on your staff, and he won't charge too much. It will add one day to the printing schedule.

SELF-MAILERS

Envelopes are hard to come by for less than two cents each, and many styles cost more. If you were to do a mailing of 5,000, the envelopes alone would cost over $100. The use of envelopes makes your mailing piece more impressive, but it is an expense you may choose to avoid, by designing the direct-mail piece as a "self-mailer."

The simplest self-mailer is a postcard. If you take a piece of double-sized postcard stock and fold it over once, you have four sides. One of the sides becomes the address side—the mailing front. The same can be true of the larger letter-sized piece, folded over once or three times. One side is the mailing side; no envelope is required.

You can staple a self-mailer, but check with the post office first to make sure the pieces are sized, prepared and fastened to their current specifications.

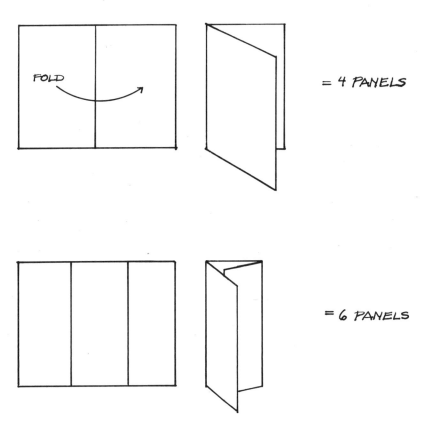

THE RETURN CARD

A separate post-paid reply card is usually included in a mailing that goes in a separate envelope. It is also possible to include as part of a self-mailing postcard. One half is the mailing front and its opposite side, with your message. The other half is made up as a separate postcard, with your name and address on its front panel and the reply coupon for the customer to fill out on its other side.

The return card half should be separated from the other half by a dotted line so the customer is invited to tear it off, fill it in and mail it back. The dotted line can also be scored by the printer so that the card tears off neatly. Scoring will not add a great deal to your cost, but it will add another day to the printing schedule.

You also have the option of perforating the dotted line. Supermarket coupons are often perforated, and easy to tear out. Those with only a dotted line require scissors to cut neatly. Perforating may add more to your costs than you choose to spend, but do check with the printer on its cost. Everything you can afford to do for the convenience of the prospective customer is valuable.

THE RETURN MAIL PERMIT

Are you going to ask your prospective customer to pay the postage for the postcard you want her to mail back? If you do, it will discourage some from returning the card.

To pay the postage yourself, fill out an application for a return mail permit at your local post office. By paying an annual accounting fee and making a deposit for the postage due, you will be assigned a permit number. The permit number should then be printed on the return card.

BULK MAIL PERMITS

Bulk mail permits are not the same as return mail permits. The bulk mail privilege enables the user to mail large quantities of mail at a reduced rate. A minimum number of pieces is required for each mailing, and they must be sorted, bundled and stickered by zip code or carrier route according to certain rules. Be sure to check with the post office on how to do this correctly.

OTHER COSTS

The costs of writing, designing and preparing your direct mail piece for the printer are important. Perhaps you can do it yourself, along with some help from the printer. If you employ a freelance writer and designer, make certain that you have a clear agreement, preferably in writing, on extra charges for reworking—and what is to be paid if you don't use the material at all.

There are other costs involved in a direct mail campaign. Someone must put the labels onto the envelopes or self-mailers; stuff the envelopes, add the postage, sort, tie and sticker the bundles for a bulk mailing, and take them to the post office.

These are time-consuming chores, and even if someone on your staff does it, it costs you for their time, and takes them away from their regular work. If you don't want to do it yourself, mailing service agencies (informally called "lettershops") will do it for you. Plan ahead for this; don't find yourself delaying the mailing while you hunt for someone to do the mailing work.

If you are going to do the mailing yourself, and don't have a postage meter, be sure to get one. Pitney-Bowes is the company to call. They will rent you the machine by the month. When it needs money added to its meter, you take that part of the machine to the post office to reset it; you must take along a check made out to the postmaster for the amount of postage you want.

Besides the operating convenience (can you imagine licking 5,000 stamps?), the cost of postage-meter rental as well as postage is deductible as a business expense, and records are easy to keep.

HOW MANY PEOPLE WILL RESPOND?

According to direct mail experts, you can expect replies from one to three percent of the names you mail. From your 5,000 pieces mailed, therefore, you can expect 150 replies at most.

Don't you believe it. These figures are industry averages. There are plenty of direct mail pieces that pull a far larger return.

For the moment, however, let's work with 3%. Say you do a postcard mailing of 5,000 which costs you $2,500. You receive 150 expressions of interest. If half of them become customers, you have gathered 75 new customers for your $2,500. That's a cost of $30 per customer.

Whether a new customer is worth $30 depends on how much each customer spends on average, and what the profit margin is, but for many businesses it's a worthwhile cost. Also, if more than half your leads become customers, the cost for each is less.

Let's compare this with what you might get from a newspaper ad: In any of the 20 largest cities of the country, a two-column ad four or five inches deep will cost about $300. At this rate, you could run the ad eight times for your $2,500. Will you get 75 new customers? That's an average of nine new customers with each running of the ad.

Only running the ad will tell you if this average is realistic to expect. Any ad may deliver the average the first time it is run. But it may not continue to deliver the average each time it is run. The last time you run it, it may be old hat, or the offer has expired.

Perhaps you can afford to advertise both ways. This would increase the public reaction. Better yet, the ad will give them the news and the mailer will act as a reminder.

Direct mail is particularly successful when it is sent to a carefully targeted audience via a select list. If you sell to a general population, it is difficult to make direct mail pay. Even for an efficient mailing piece, the overall cost may be more than many small businesses can handle. If you sell to the general public, a simple mailing to a zip-code list near your store is probably best.

11

Co-op Advertising

Many large companies offer their retailers and dealers several forms of cooperative (co-op) advertising to encourage the retailers to promote their products. Some manufacturers offer this selling aid only a couple of times a year; others provide it on a continuing basis.

The most interesting offer they make to encourage you to promote their products is money. Or the chance to spend less of it when you advertise their product in the advertising of your store.

The manufacturer will always require you to prove you actually spent the agreed amount of money when you ask them for reimbursement. And they always put a limit on how much money they will contribute.

In any event, the manufacturer's sales staff or distributors should advise you of the availability of cop-op funds. They may not offer it. Ask for it. More than a few manufacturers provide it only to those retailers who request it!

IN-STORE MATERIAL

Usually, manufacturers will not only offer display material to dress up your store with their product name, they will beg you to use it. Use it if you possibly can. It will give your store a "new look" (as long as you don't continue displaying it long after it gets shopworn).

This material is called "point of sale" promotion and can do a great job of stimulating sales. It is particularly useful if tied in with your newspaper advertising, because the customer sees your ad promoting the item and then sees it promoted again when she visits your store.

NEWSPAPER CO-OP ADVERTISING

Another co-op offer many manufacturers make is to provide you with fully prepared newspaper ads. All you have to do is hand the material over to the newspaper and instruct the newspaper to insert your store name and address, etc., in the indicated area.

Newspaper co-op material is usually provided in a variety of sizes, ranging from small space to very large space. You can run the size you choose. This material can save you money, particularly if the ad contains artwork which would be expensive for you to prepare. In most cases it is done in a highly professional manner.

Many manufacturers will offer co-op funds—their offer to pay for part of the ad—if you have run an ad they have prepared. Don't miss out on the chance for reimbursement just because you choose to run your ad instead of theirs.

When a small business like yours runs co-op material, the manufacturer benefits because the manufacturer's image is protected by eliminating the possibility of some small store producing a sleazy ad to promote the product.

Both the manufacturer and the retailer benefit from co-op advertising, and you should take every advantage of it you can.

12

The Yellow Pages

If you are planning on opening a business, the first thing you should do is plan your yellow pages (telephone directory) advertising. The reason for this is that you can place this advertising only once during the year, and the "closing date" is different for every book. In some cases, such as a market where there is a metropolitan edition plus one or more suburban editions, the dates of closing differ for each directory. Get on it right away: you should have it placed by the time you sign the lease for your store.

If your business is already open, read this chapter and then take a moment or two to review your yellow pages advertising program. If, after reading this chapter, you feel there is something better you can do, do it now even if the next book is not going to be published for six or seven months. Take your time in preparing both your schedule of sizes and the material that will go in the book. Look at how you compare with the competition. Be confident of your plans far ahead of the "closing dates" because they almost never can be delayed.

WHICH "YELLOW PAGES" DO YOU USE?

Yes, there is more than one. Anyone can publish a telephone directory and print it on yellow paper if they wish. The newcomers make an apparent effort to look as much like the original as possible.

The only thing any yellow pages directory can offer you is circulation. If a yellow pages company trying to sell you space does not have 100% circulation in your area, you should not consider them, even though they may be cheaper than the yellow pages published by the telephone company.

If a salesman tells you they plan to have 100% circulation or they expect to have it, you don't have much of a guarantee that every home in your neighborhood will actually receive a directory carrying your advertising.

The yellow pages telephone directory published by your local telephone company has the name of the telephone company right on the cover. Among the first couple of pages in the directory there will be a notice of where to call for information about advertising in the yellow pages. Call them and ask for a salesman to visit you now. Even if the closing date is nine months away and the salesman tells you there is plenty of time, you want to see him now. You want to learn the rates for various sizes of space and the coverage of the various directories and you want to plan your advertising for the next issue early.

It may take more than one directory to cover the area you want to reach with your ad. The rates for the directories are all different, depending on the circulation of each directory.

Few if any telephone companies publish a formal rate card the way newspapers and radio and television stations do. But the salesman will have something in writing regarding the various sizes and their costs.

YELLOW PAGES SIZES

You cannot buy any size you want in yellow pages the way you can with newspapers. The sizes are standard but there is a large variety to choose from. Unfortunately, the telephone company assigns mysterious identifications to these sizes,

MULTIPLE LISTINGS

You may find that your competition uses one basic heading and then uses a very small ad (or perhaps just a one-line listing) in a secondary heading. This secondary listing will also carry the words "Please see our ad on page 000." Such a reference is free when you appear in a second category, and—it is hoped—makes the reader turn to your big ad in another section. It is certainly cheaper than running a big ad in two sections and it's the way many people do it.

The important point is that, if your competition appears in two sections, you should appear in those same two sections. Match the competition every way you can.

BOLD LISTINGS

When you buy space in the yellow pages, you are not charged for the regular listing. But if you want that listing to appear in bold (heavy, dark) type you will pay a small extra charge. Go for it. It's worth it. Use a Bold Listing in the White Pages, too. Like the directory listing in the Yellow Pages, this listing (in regular type) is free. The use of bold will add a small charge, but it's also worth it.

13

Transit Advertising

Transit advertising are those cards you see on the inside of buses, trolley cars and subways. It includes the cards on the outside of the cars, too, and the ones at the bus stop. One of the great advantages of transit advertising is that you can buy space on only the cars that run past or near your store. If your store is on Bus Route Number Five, you can buy the buses that run on that line only and so, theoretically, your message is going to only those people who might visit your store conveniently.

There is a problem with that promise. On occasion, a bus or car will be re-routed so it runs on a different line for a day or a week or more! Your message is being delivered out in the sticks some where where it does you no good at all. This does not happen a great deal, but it does happen and you should know it up front. You will also not usually get any money back for this "administrative hitch."

In order to investigate transit advertising, look up the transit company in your white pages. The exact name of the company will appear somewhere on the bus. Call them and tell them you want to talk to transit advertising sales department. The salesman will come to visit you and discuss the different routes available and the cost for each one.

You will be buying the right to put cards on all the buses on whatever line or lines you buy. The more bus lines you buy, the cheaper it gets for each one. It's just like newspaper lines or radio and television spots—cheaper by the dozen.

You have to print the signs exactly to the size and paper weight the transit company tells you to. They will also tell you how many to print. The printer delivers them to the transit company, which puts them on the correct buses.

Transit advertising is usually sold in blocks of 30-day "showings," which means a calendar month. There are some transit companies that sell only 60-day or 90-day showings—particularly on popular routes such as the ones that run right through downtown.

Transit advertising is almost always printed on coated stock, which is paper that looks to have been varnished so the rain and snow won't destroy it. It isn't cheap. The cost is added to by the fact that you won't be printing many cards—perhaps 50 or 75. Further, you'll probably want to use color, so the cost of preparation may boggle your mind.

PRINTING TRANSIT CARDS

Get a bid from your friendly neighborhood printer—the one who does your stationery and other things. If he doesn't do this kind of work, he will be glad to recommend someone who does do it.

The transit company itself can prepare the cards for you in many cases. Ask their price, too. It's often a good idea for you to have the transit company to prepare the cards in case there is a goof-up somewhere in the printing. They would bend over backwards to get the job re-printed in time for the "showing." An outside printer may not only give you an argument over whose fault the error is; he may tell you it is impossible to get the job done over again in time for the showing.

INSIDE OR OUTSIDE?

You know that you can advertise inside the bus as well as on the outside. You can even buy two "showings" inside the bus—two cards facing each other so people sitting on either side of the bus can read your message. Cards on the inside get a lot of attention because people are on a bus for more than a few minutes with very little to do or look at. On the other hand, a card on the outside gets far more exposure from its travel past so many people on the street and in cars and on bicycles. Which is better? Forget "research." The answer is complicated and may not apply to your business at all. Do what your common sense tells you to do.

DOES TRANSIT ADVERTISING WORK?

Obviously, there is a benefit or so many people would not use it. There is no doubt that it is good "reminder" advertising. It may not be the best way to advertise a sale which ends in a week or two. Generally, it is not efficient for anything that requires prompt action from the prospect. It does get your name around your neighborhood.

In New York City, many Broadway shows use transit advertising. That practice is not much older than 25 years. Previously no Broadway show would use transit advertising because it was felt that the people who ride subways do not go to the theatre, where tickets today can run as high as $50 each.

But a Broadway producer wanted to advertise somewhere that other Broadway shows did not advertise. He chose transit advertising and put cards on the subways. He made history. The show became a hit and ran for years. Much of the credit for that was given to the job done by transit advertising. Now it's used frequently, even for opera!

Perhaps transit advertising should be one of the last things you spend your advertising dollars on, because you need all the money you can spare for media advertising such as radio, television and newspapers—to say nothing of direct mail. After you have satisfied that need, you may wish to consider transit advertising. At least you know what it is now and how to do it.

14

"Free" Advertising

There is no such thing as "free" advertising. Period. Anyone should know that when the smartest minds in marketing spend billions of dollars in advertising each year, world-wide, they do it only because they have to. If advertising could be got free, don't you think the big boys would do it? Of course they would. Yet sharp hustlers keep coming up with one new scheme after the other which promises free advertising.

These schemes are never offered to large advertisers, who are far too sophisticated to even listen to the sales pitch. Such "plans" are offered to small-business owners who may be naive enough to participate.

The gimmicks designed to provide you with free advertising take many forms. The basic selling point of many of these schemes is, "This is an entirely new concept."

THE DISCOUNT COUPON BOOK

This is one of the oldest of the free advertising concepts. Usually, this concept identifies itself as a "club." The first thing the organizer does is to line up small businesses in your neighborhood to participate. A big feature of this plan is little work for you to do and no expense to you.

You sign an agreement promising that you will honor the discount coupons "The Club" prints. The coupon for your business promises 25% off, or half off, or whatever. The customer simply comes to your store and automatically gets a discount on the cost of your product or service. It will cost you nothing.

Of course, it does cost you something. If you give 25% off on a $10 purchase, you are spending $2.50 to get that customer to buy your product. On a $50 purchase, you are spending $12.50 to get that sale.

What you really have is a 25% A/S (advertising to sales) ratio. A 25% A/S ratio is very high if you have budgeted 10-15% of your revenue for advertising. It's costing you ten percent more than your normal advertising does. So, where is the "free" advertising? It doesn't exist.

Worse: There are many small businesses which cannot afford to give 25% or more off on every purchase. A restaurant, for example, which does good business on Thursday, Friday and Saturday nights does not have any need to give 25% off on those nights to fill the room. They only need help Monday through Wednesday.

If you limit your offer to Monday through Wednesday, you are going to annoy a lot of potential customers and you may wind up losing more than you will gain.

What do you do with a customer who comes in on a Saturday night, has a splendid dinner and hands you a coupon for 25% off when you give him his check? You tell him the coupon is no good on Saturday night. Now he hates you and may never come back. The fact that the coupon says "Not good on Saturdays" means nothing to the customer. He will be even more angry that he didn't see that.

The same would apply to beauty parlors or auto or television repair stores. Most likely, you won't be able to offer 25% off on everything. There's just too much opportunity for misunderstanding and disappointment on the part of your customers.

The discount coupon technique probably has some merit for fast-food operations. But most of them do their own coupon printing and distribution, so their coupons are not in a book with 100 or more other coupons.

More than a few of the coupon clubs will charge you a service charge or a printing fee or something just to appear in their book. Still, they claim to be providing you with "free" advertising. It isn't free by any means—no matter how you look at it.

SELF-LIQUIDATING ADVERTISING

Doesn't that sound professional? ... And promising ... And provocative? It's a fine sounding phrase. The trouble is that the phrase describes just one more gimmick that masquerades as advertising. What is it?

You've seen plenty of it. It's the T-shirt with the name of the restaurant on it. The baseball cap with the name of the gas station on it. Etc., etc. If you buy T-shirts with your store's advertising message on them and give them away, you're asking for a big expense to achieve very little.

First of all, you have to buy the T-shirts. Now what are you going to do with them? Give them away with a purchase? You're going to have to advertise that! Seems like a lot of money and effort to get your name on a T-shirt.

Where does the "self-liquidating" come in? That's easy. You pay $6 for each T-shirt you get from the manufacturer. You sell them to your customers for $6 and the T-shirt costs you nothing. Isn't that wonderful! At least that's what the T-shirt salesman will tell you.

Why go into the T-shirt business?

Forget it. Put your advertising dollars into established advertising methods. Don't put it into gimmicks.

The only exception is ballpoint pens. You can get them for about ten cents each with your name on them. You're going to have to have them for your business anyway and your customers will walk away with them. That's a nice, inexpensive way to use "self-liquidating" advertising!

15

Your Advertising Budget

At the beginning of this book, we told you that you must advertise if you are going to lead your competition. Certainly there are more than a few businesses which do not advertise at all. There are also more than a few businesses which fail. There are many, many more which stay alive but complain they "can't afford" to advertise.

YOU CAN'T AFFORD NOT TO ADVERTISE!

You should invest at least ten percent of your total income in advertising. When money is tight, it is very tempting to take the position that you'll advertise next week or next month but you can't afford it right now.

You must consider advertising a basic expense like rent or salaries or electricity. You don't save money on advertising by not doing it. You simply eliminate a selling tool, and your business will be less because of it. The way to save money on advertising is to make it cost-efficient.

It may be that your particular business will require an advertising expenditure of less than 10% of your total income. It may also be that it will take 15% to meet the competition. You answer the question, "How much?" by starting with a figure—say 10%—and then adjusting it to meet your needs.

IF YOUR BUSINESS IS ALREADY IN OPERATION

What was your total (gross) income last year? Whatever it was, you probably want to do more in the coming year. Plan on an increase for the upcoming year in your total business income and add that increase to the total amount you did last year. Now you have your "marketing goal."

Do not plan on your business going down. Do not plan on it staying at the same level, either. You must plan for growth because running in place is losing. No matter what becomes of the economy, no matter what new competition has appeared, you must find ways to do more business each year. Advertising can help you do that.

If you are purchasing an existing business, you should do the same kind of planning. Take the amount of sales they had for the year before you took over and add to it the amount of additional sales you realistically believe you can generate. That is your marketing goal.

HOW TO SET UP YOUR ADVERTISING BUDGET

Put it in writing! Don't take the attitude that you have so little money for advertising it isn't worth the time and effort to write it down. No matter if it's $100 a week, if you multiply it by 52 weeks, you're over $5,000. Spending that amount of money is worth planning.

As a matter of fact, the less money you have, the more it's true that you should work from a written budget. With little cash available, overspending is a serious offense and it's very easy to order newspaper ads or radio commercials thinking you surely can afford a small investment to promote a sale next Saturday. The bill for it will always come at the wrong time unless you've planned your advertising budget.

If you're going to put it in writing, where do you start? For most any business or service, a budget should be in two parts: continuing advertising and promotional advertising. A continuing budget provides for a continuing program—52 weeks a year with no breaks except for extraordinary circumstances such as the period immediately following the Christmas holidays (if that circumstance applies to your business). Yellow pages advertising would be an example of your continuing advertising program.

A promotional budget provides for promotions during the year when you simply must increase your regular advertising schedule: periods such as Christmas holidays and seasonal promotions such as spring, summer, fall and winter. If you're in the carpet-cleaning business, spring cleaning is an ideal time to make that extra-heavy push. If you're in the furniture reupholstery business, October and November are vital months to advertise strongly because so many people want to do something in time for their holiday entertaining.

Whatever your business, you'll be able to plan in an overall fashion for the times of the year that you want to do more than normal advertising. These times are your promotional advertising campaigns.

Which items do you write down first? Promotional or continuing? In most cases, you should plan your promotional budget first. These are times of the year when you must do your strongest selling and that means you must do your strongest advertising at these times, too.

But there are items in the continuing advertising budget which you cannot do without. Items such as yellow pages and its monthly cost cannot be cut back in any one month.

So, actually, you plan both the promotional and continuing budget at the same time. List the things you must do and then the things you want to do, and see if you come anywhere near staying within your budget. Good luck. If you stay within your allocation, you're one of the few marketers who have been able to do it the first time you plan.

There is nothing wrong with revising your budget—you can revise it the minute you have finished preparing it and you can revise it as your business year progresses.

Do not throw your previous (outdated) budgets away. Save them for reference later to see how much you had to revise to meet the conditions of the market and to guide you in preparing a future year's activity. Be sure to put a date on your budget showing when you prepared it so you'll know which version was prepared when.

On the next two pages is a sample budget form. You can expand on it or eliminate those items you do not use. Start with this one and develop one that is particularly useful for your business.

ADVERTISING BUDGET FOR THE YEAR _____

(DATE PREPARED _____)

Total projected gross sales $_____
Ad budget at 10% of sales $_____
Ad budget at 15% of sales $_____

CONTINUING ADVERTISING EXPENSES

Yellow pages @ $_____ per mo. $_____

Newspaper advertising
52 Insertions of 150 lines $_____

Radio advertising
12 spots per week/26 weeks $_____
Commercial preparation $_____

TV advertising
6 spots per week/13 weeks $_____
Commercial preparation $_____

TOTAL COST OF
CONTINUING ADVERTISING
        $_____

PROMOTIONAL ADVERTISING EXPENSES

Direct mail advertising

Prepare 4-pp/1-color piece $ _ _ _ _ _ _ _ _ _ _

Print 5,000 pieces $ _ _ _ _ _ _ _ _ _ _

Postage @_____ each $ _ _ _ _ _ _ _ _ _ _

TOTAL DIRECT MAIL COST $ _ _ _ _ _ _ _ _ _ _

Newspaper advertising

Six "sale" promotions $ _ _ _ _ _ _ _ _ _ _

Christmas advertising $ _ _ _ _ _ _ _ _ _ _

Other promotions (itemize):

TOTAL ANNUAL COST OF
PROMOTIONAL ADVERTISING

        $ _ _ _ _ _ _ _ _ _ _

TOTAL ADVERTISING
BUDGET FOR THE YEAR

        $ _ _ _ _ _ _ _ _ _ _

16

Creative Concepts
for Success

No matter who does your creative work—you yourself, an advertising agency, the newspaper, the television or radio station—good creative work does not start with the writing.

COMPETITIVE ADVERTISING

All good creative work begins with a thorough knowledge of your competitors' advertising. You must know what the competition is selling, how much is being charged, the services offered, etc.

To achieve this, buy a scrapbook and collect competitive advertising. It will become your best guide as to what to do—and not to do. When you clip a newspaper ad, be sure to clip the day of publication and the name of the publication (or write it alongside the ad) so you can later review the material.

You will not be able to collect radio or television commercials for your scrapbook, but you can jot down the concept of the commercial and put it in your book, along with the date you heard or saw it and the station on which it was broadcast.

For direct mail pieces, call your competitors and ask for a catalog or brochure or whatever it is they offer. Pretend you are a prospective customer and have them send it to your home address. To make sure you remain anonymous, you may have it sent to the home of a friend or relative.

If you were able to afford the services of a reputable and talented advertising agency, that is where they would start. They do nothing until they have a collection of competitors' advertising. You should start there too.

"LET'S DO A NEW AD!"

Wrong. The first person to get tired of your advertising will be you or your wife or your partner. If your ad is not promoting a sale or a limited-time offer, keep it going.

There are more than a few large national advertisers who have been running the same ad for more than ten years! This may seem an exaggeration but it is true. Further, some of these long-lasting ads are "direct response." They have a coupon in the ad so the advertiser knows, month to month, if the ad is still working.

This phenomenon illustrates the classic question asked by the title of this book, "Did you see my ad?"

"No." Advertisers who spend thousands of dollars a month on one ad, rerunning it month after month, are flabbergasted by this response, but it happens.

The only test is: Does the ad get results and does it continue to get results? If it does, don't change it. Resist the temptation to change the photo of that girl in the illustration of your ad. You may think you are replacing her with a more attractive girl, but you won't know that until you run the ad.

Old sayings become old sayings by being true. Here's one of the truest: *If it ain't broke, don't fix it!*

ONE MEDIUM VERSUS THE MEDIA

There are advertisers who get "hooked" on one medium and use it exclusively for an extended period of time. They go on radio or television or in the newspaper. If it works, they just stay with it.

Sounds reasonable but it isn't. These same people compound the error. Having devoted a long period of time in one medium, they give another medium only a half-hearted try. If it does not immediately surpass what they have been doing, they abandon it and return to the proven formula.

If you are a small advertiser with very little advertising dollars, that may be the only thing you think you can do. There is little point in continuing to invest dollars in newspapers if they are delivering no customers when your radio advertising is doing a good job for you.

Consider the many people out there who never read a newspaper and the many people who never turn on the radio. It may be hard to believe they exist but, they do.

Your job is to reach everyone in your marketing area and you will do it best with a combination of media rather than just one.

You don't have to use all of them at the same time. You can be on radio one month, television the next, and newspapers the third month. Then return to radio for the fourth month.

You can't afford to support failure advertising, but if any one medium does not appear to work at all, don't just assume the medium is no good for your business. Look to other possible reasons you failed: Your message was not effective. The time you went on the air was wrong to reach your target market.

"ME TOO" ADVERTISING

You must be careful not to be an echo of your competition. In many businesses, this is difficult, because you are all selling the same thing—gasoline or maternity clothes or vacuum cleaners. You may be selling the same thing but the look and the tone and the style of your advertising can be different. You can seem to be a store the prospect would rather do business with.

MULTI-CLAIM VERSUS SINGLE-CLAIM ADVERTISING

Among professionals the argument of multi-claim versus single-claim advertising gets heated. The fact is that both approaches work—sometimes.

It will be very tempting in preparing your advertising to list all the reasons the prospect should come to you. Is it convenience, quality, price, location, or impulse that brings the prospect to your door?   Not always easy to determine. Consequently, it is tempting to give the prospect every reason you can think of to do business with you.

The fact is that you will be taking up valuable space in your small ad to list advantages that may be of little importance to the majority of your prospects. You may turn these people off before they read the one reason in your ad that would have delivered them to your doorstep.

Rather than do one ad (or commercial) which talks about convenience, quality, price and location, why not do an ad that devotes most of its thrust to just one of those advantages? That will give you the opportunity to do four different ads. Of course, you can mention more than one advantage of doing business with your store but put the emphasis on just one claim.

Fine. Now—which advantage should you talk about in your first ad?

PRE-EMPT THE CLAIM

If you make a claim for your product or service which is also true for the competition—but he is not making that claim— you can pre-empt the claim as a selling point for you. You will be the only one saying it.

Such claims as "No charge for delivery," or "Open till nine every day," may be true for your competitor but if you are the only one saying it, it will be impressive.

By the time your competition catches on and begins making the same claim, you will have changed your ad to feature some other advantage that sets you apart. Your competitor will be left running "me too" advertising and it won't get him many customers.

"PICTURE OF THE FACTORY" ADVERTISING

An unforgivable and very normal thing to do is to present features about your product or service which cost you a big sum of money. You want the public to know you spent it, but they don't really care. This is called "picture of the factory" advertising, because the classic example is an ad which shows a $2 million factory built to make the product.

Who cares? The public is tough. All it cares about is

What have you got?

How good is it?

What does it cost?

If you take over a restaurant and invest $100,000 in renovations, it's a fine copy approach to tell the public that you have given the old place a whole new look. Don't tell them what you spent. They know you expect to make your money back from them!

The point your copy should make is not that you spent a lot of money. The point is what you have done for your customers. A fine point but an important one in selling.

POP LINGO

Be careful of popular, new language expressions in your advertising. A hot one these days is "state of the art." It means up to date, the latest model. It's an empty claim which anyone can make. The state of the art today may be old hat tomorrow. And besides, maybe I don't have to have the latest model, particularly if I can save a bundle by buying last year's perfectly good one.

"TEASER" ADVERTISING

The best thing about teaser advertising is that it's cute. What a waste! You are usually only "teasing" your sales and wasting your valuable advertising dollars running an ad that says:

WATCH FOR BIG NEWS ABOUT
SEWING MACHINES NEXT MONDAY

Do you really think anyone is going to do that? Of course not.

Yet every once in a while and more often than is smart, someone will run a teaser campaign. You've seen it. Don't do it.

THE LOGO

General Electric is but one of the large, multi-national companies that has a logo. You could show the GE in a circle to people, young and old, all over the world and they would tell you it refers to General electric. A logo can be a very valuable selling tool because it can set your advertising apart from the competition. It's like a monogram.

If you choose to develop a logo, be sure to include it in all your public communication—your newspaper, magazine, direct-mail, radio and television advertising, your business cards, your store window—use it everywhere you can think of. The more you use it, the more valuable it becomes.

Where do you get a logo? You'll have to hire an artist or design agency unless you are an artist yourself. That will cost you somewhere between $100 and $500,000.

Find a local store with a logo of their own—not one established by a national company. Check the yellow pages and watch for service trucks which might carry the owner's logo. Call them up and ask them who did their logo. They may even tell you what they paid for it.

When you find an artist who will develop a logo for you, at the kind of investment you are willing to make, get his complete terms in writing.

For example: What if he designs three logos and offers you a choice but you don't like any of them? Have you committed yourself to an expense for nothing? You may have.

All artists maintain a portfolio of their completed work. Ask to see it. If you like what he or she has done for other companies, chances are you will get something that satisfies you.

Make certain you *really* like it, because you are going to have to live with it for a long time. If you get tired of it, the only thing you can do is abandon it. That's a waste of money and opportunity. And about the worst thing you can do is change your logo.

When a logo is developed for you and you pay for it, do you "own" it? Maybe not, unless the letter of agreement says you do. Some artists merely "rent" you the right to use their artwork. This is a bad thing for you. You may find that when you want to sell your business, you don't own your logo!

Things to get in writing :
1. You own the logo.
2. The number of different choices you will be given.
3. For reproduction purposes, will the art be suitable for color or black and white? Or both?
4. If you reject all efforts, what do you pay?
5. What is the total cost of the job, including "finished art," ready for reproduction in newspapers or direct mail?

DO YOU NEED A SLOGAN?

Of course, you do. A slogan is a theme, a statement about how you do business, a catchy phrase explaining your superiority over the competition. It alone will not deliver sales, but it does give you individuality. "Thank You, Paine Webber," and "AT&T, the more you listen, the better we sound," are interesting examples. The first is really nothing more than a polite expression. But it implies that you will have something to thank them for if you do business with them. The AT&T slogan clearly implies superiority.

The most important contribution of a slogan is that it never wears out. The more you use it, the better it gets and the better you are known. The only mistake you can make is to not use it at all time. For example, can you make it part of your logo, or the sign over your store or on your store window? Is it on your letterhead and your notepaper and your merchandise receipts and estimate forms? Paint it on your truck and, yes, incorporate it in your personalized license plates if you can.

17

"Did You See My Ad?"

"No." You read that joke earlier, but it's worth repeating because it is very discouraging to run an ad and learn that not many of your friends saw it. Forget it. It doesn't mean anything. This type of "survey" is called "mother-in-law research" and is totally invalid.

There are bound to be people who did not see your ad this morning. You may find that having been in the newspaper every week for a month will still present you with customers who never saw your advertising before. They came to see you because a friend recommended you. That does not mean the ad isn't working.

If a newspaper has a circulation of half a million, don't think half a million people will read your ad tomorrow morning. Many of them won't read any part of the newspaper, and plenty of them who do will miss your ad.

The real question is: Over a period of time, how many customers have been delivered to you as a result of your advertising? Even if that figure is less than you would wish for, you must consider another factor. If your competition is appearing in the newspaper, you really should combat that effort in the same newspaper, if you possibly can. High visibility is a key factor in any successful marketing effort.

EVERYTHING WORKS

No one has ever been able to prove there is a product which can not be sold in any media. For years, established professionals in the field of advertising stated flatly that department stores could not use television successfully. As a viewer today, you know that is not true. The only thing that has changed is that department stores and their advertising agencies have learned how to do it.

One of the country's largest trade schools currently gets most of its leads by sending a direct-mail/direct-response postcard to prospects, asking them to "Call now!" For more than ten years this chain of schools relied on television and newspapers alone, feeling that direct mail didn't work for them. It does work. They just weren't using it right.

So don't be quick to say, "Newspapers (or radio or television) don't work for me." You can be successful in a medium no matter what your product or service. If you are not successful, you are not making the right offer in an appealing way to your potential customers.

THE CUMULATIVE EFFECT

It is difficult for any business which maintains a regular advertising program to know exactly where the customers come from. Did they come into the store because of a newspaper ad, a radio commercial or a direct-mail piece?

When a store asks a customer, "How did you hear about us?" and gets the answer, "Oh, I've always known about you," it may be discouraging. You want to know if your newspaper ad is working. But don't frown! What the customer just proved is that *all* your advertising is working.

You may be a merchant but you're a customer, too. How many times have you seen someone's advertising for a long period of time but did not react to it simply because you were not in the market for that product at that time? Then the day comes when you need that kind of product, and you turn to the yellow pages to find someone who sells it.

Now you go to the store because of the yellow pages ad but, really, that store has been courting your business ever since the first day you saw their newspaper ad or heard their radio commercial and did nothing about it.

This is what is known as "cumulative effect." It is an established, valid advertising concept. If you give all the credit to the yellow pages in the above example, you are ignoring the cumulative effect. Of course, your yellow pages ad did its job. But other advertising did its job, too.

The behavior pattern we have cited which applies to you as a consumer applies to consumers of your product or service. Diversify your advertising budget as much as you can in order to be in as much of the media as possible. Newspapers bolster radio advertising and radio bolsters television and they all give your direct mail more credibility. It all works.

18

Let's Write an Ad!

As you begin to read this chapter, I'm going to assume you have read all the chapters that came before it. If you have, congratulations!

Now what do you do?

If you haven't been able to find an advertising agency to prepare your newspaper advertising and/or you don't like what the local newspaper has prepared for you, you may want to write your own ad.

Every first-rate copywriter once sat down at a typewriter to face that challenge that makes writers want to consider suicide—the blank page of paper in the typewriter.

Have courage. Your first ad may well be a winner. More than a few good writers look back on the first ad they ever wrote with considerable pride. It doesn't have to be amateurish failure. If you have read the previous chapters of this book, you have already learned some "rules" that will give you a good shot at success. If you have read this book, you have already learned more than some highly paid copywriters know.

REVIEW COMPETITIVE MATERIAL

Your first step is to get out the competition's advertising you have been collecting. Tape it on the wall in front of your desk or some handy place where you can constantly look at it. You must be different. Not only in your "look" but in your claims and the reasons you give the prospect to come to your store.

SELECT AD SIZE

The size of your ad will have some bearing on how much you can say. Hopefully, your budget will allow you to prepare an ad as large as your competitor's. Let's assume that is the case.

Now, look at the competitor's ad. Does it look crowded? If it does, is it because there are too many words or is it because the illustration or the headline or some other element is too large?

What if it looks pretty good? Then you must not use more words than he has, or your ad will look crowded, and it will probably have too much for the reader to absorb.

You will be checking competitive advertising constantly as you prepare your ad, making certain that you are communicating more by saying less. That is your aim.

WRITE THE HEADLINE

The largest words in your ad. The "grabber" that makes people stop and read. The big news that is going to make the customer come to your store today.

For the sake of this exercise, assume that your business is furniture reupholstery. The month is February and not a big one for sales in this business. Potential customers are dealing with bills left over from the holiday season that just ended. Furniture reupholstery is an expensive project that people can put off for a few months. You want them to buy now. Begin writing!

Jot down on a pad some sample headlines like these:

REUPHOLSTER NOW!
QUALITY REUPHOLSTERING
REUPHOLSTER ON A BUDGET

CHICAGO'S LEADING REUPHOLSTERING SHOP
REUPHOLSTERY—CHICAGO'S LARGEST
FABRIC SELECTION

Let's look at those headlines for a moment. The first one tells the customer to do something we already suspect she can't afford. Not a good headline.

The second headline claims quality work. Not a bad idea but, again, she can't afford it right now.

The third one appeals to her pocketbook, but even budget reupholstery is expensive, and the customer knows it.

The fourth headline says you're big and probably good. Again, we have not solved the customer's financial problem and therefore have not made her an offer she can't refuse.

The fifth headline assures her she is going to find the fabric she wants in our shop. Fine. When she is ready to buy she may remember us. Not a good headline for business now.

Suppose you offer the customer the chance to reupholster now but not make any payment for sixty days?

If she buys in February, her furniture won't be reupholstered until late March. If you bill her in April—60 days after she signs the order—you may be solving her financial problem somewhat and making a sale now.

So your headline becomes:

REUPHOLSTER NOW
No payments for sixty days

There's something wrong with that. "No payments for sixty days" is a sub-head. You want the visual emphasis to be on the payment offer. So your layout will look like this:

Reupholster Now!
NO PAYMENT FOR SIXTY DAYS!

Now you can hope you have made an offer the customer can't refuse. You have attacked the copy problem with a marketing solution. And you didn't even know you did it!

Sometimes you may feel you have two headlines of equal importance. Wrong. One has to be more important than the other. Be strong and tough with yourself. Your gut will tell you which is the headline. Many ads fail because they are a collection of headlines. Everything is a big statement in bold type and all caps with exclamation points (!!!!). Those writers are talking to themselves. The prospect is not impressed.

Now that you have our headline and your subhead, you are ready for

BODY COPY

The body copy is the block or blocks of words that tell your story in detail. *The body copy must support the headline.* The copy explains the headline to those prospects who are tempted by your headline but not yet sold by it. Don't ask the body copy to do more than that. If it does only that, it has done its job.

So, your body copy says:

Choose from Chicago's widest selection of quality fabrics right in your own home ...

That's wrong. It's a fine statement but it does not support the headline. You've changed the subject and your prospect will be confused. Support and explain your headline, like this:

You can reupholster now and pay nothing for sixty days! Choose from Chicago's widest selection of quality fabrics and pay nothing for sixty days.

Notice the reference to selection sneaked in, but done within the context of the headline. And it makes the offer of no payment for sixty days twice. Now, shut up! You've made your big offer.

There is only one more thing to do:

ASK FOR THE ORDER

Many a good salesman makes a fine presentation but never gets to the point where he asks, "May I take your order?" It is always the last thing you say. This is done in newspapers with

THE SIGNATURE

This is your name, address and phone number. You "sign" your ads the same way you sign a letter. If you want your prospective customer to CALL NOW, it is imperative that those words be in front of your telephone number and that they be very large, perhaps as large as your name. Of course it goes at the bottom of the ad. Don't ask at the top of your ad for the readers to call now. You haven't yet given them a reason to do it. Your body copy gives them a reason to call you, and then you end your appeal with a request to call now.

DO YOU NEED A PICTURE?

Perhaps you do, but you should not put a picture in your ad just to have one. Putting a photograph of a pretty girl in your ad just so it will get the reader's attention is not enough reason to do it. Putting a photo of a chair or sofa in your reupholstery ad would not help sell the customer on spending money now.

You pay for every bit of space in a newspaper ad. Use it wisely. If you need a picture to display your product, use it, but if you feel you can do without it, you're better off with white space.

THE FINISHED COPY

Now that you've worked out your copy, you are going to type it neatly, double or triple spaced, and give it to the newspaper art director with some guidance as to how it should look.

Do not try to do a layout yourself. The art director is better at it than you are. Also, he will probably be very happy to let you lay out the ad wrong. It's less work for him. He will appreciate your need for him and your respect for his professionalism.

But you can give him an idea of what you have in mind, as shown below.

CHICAGO TRIBUNE
COPY FOR JONES REUPHOLSTERY 2 col x 50 lines

Reupholster Now !
NO PAYMENTS FOR SIXTY DAYS!

Choose from Chicago's widest selection of quality fabrics and pay nothing for sixty days.

CALL NOW! 555-3456

Jones Reupholstery * 345 Division Street

Note: Subhead should be larger than headline.
Please lay out "call now" and phone number in largest type in ad except subhead.

If you like what has been done so far, you've made another mistake!

You have prepared an ad according to "the rules" but one with a brief, sterile message that appeals on only one level—how to pay for your service.

Now you need to add some "romance" to the ad. An illustration would soften the message, but pictures of reupholstering are about as interesting as pictures of plumbing supplies. It would probably be a waste of newspaper space.

You need more copy—something that reenforces your potential customer's natural desire to re-do that scroungy sofa or lounge chair.

Add a paragraph—just a couple of lines that won't cost much—of "romance" copy to tempt your potential customer with the results of her spending money with you.

Make your favorite furniture look as though you bought it yesterday! Make your home look new again.

Now the ad copy will be like this:

Reupholster Now!
NO PAYMENTS FOR SIXTY DAYS!

Choose from Chicago's widest selection of quality fabrics and pay nothing for sixty days.

Make your favorite furniture look as though you bought it yesterday! Make your home look new again.

CALL NOW! 555-6635
Jones Reupholstery * 465 Division Street

"I CAN WRITE A BETTER AD THAN THAT"

Sure you can. The example makes no pretense of being earth-shaking. It is a simple, straightforward presentation of an offer (you hope) the consumer cannot refuse.

It does include the elements that work towards making an ad efficient, which are:

1. A headline that is the best you can devise to stop the reader and make her think about your product or service.
2. Body copy which supports the headline.
3. Additional copy only if it continues to support the headline.

19

The Ten Commandments

Whether he is selling a service or a product, any merchant feels a sense of genuine achievement when his advertising produces customers. If your advertising does not deliver customers, you are doing it wrong. It is my hope that the information in this book will help you to do it right.

I have spelled out a lot of "rules." But I told you in the beginning that rules were made to be broken. However, there are certain things that you really must do if you are going to be successful. They are rules that should *not* be broken. For every successful advertiser there must be a dozen who fail in their advertising efforts. Many of them retreat to a position of not doing any advertising. They are making a tragic mistake. They simply are not following the rules.

There are ten guidelines covered in this book which are so important that you should consider them to be virtual "commandments." They are recapped here so you can learn them. They will save you a lot of money and a lot of wasted effort.

1. KEEP TRACK OF COMPETITIVE ADVERTISING

Begin a file of advertising done by your competition and keep it up to date. The older it becomes, the more valuable it becomes. Don't try to remember what your competition did last Christmas or last Fourth of July. Look at your file and get some insight as to what he did last year. Check it against what you are doing now. Be constantly aware of his changes in media selection so you can fight him on his own turf.

2. PREPARE AN ANNUAL BUDGET

Either follow the form provided in the chapter on budgeting or dream one up yourself, but work from a written budget. When you have a reason to change it, write up a new one and give it a new date or a revision number. Keep all the budgets in your file, because later planning will benefit from reviewing the history of what you did as opposed to what you planned to do.

3. PUT ALL ADVERTISING ORDERS IN WRITING

Whether you are hiring an artist for a logo or ordering newspaper space, put it in writing. Not only will this prevent any misunderstanding about what you have agreed to do, it will give you a written record of what you have done. When the bill comes in, you can compare it with the order. You'll be surprised by how many large, reputable companies will mistakenly over-bill for services rendered.

4. DEVELOP A LOGO AND A SLOGAN

And use them at all times. The fact that you and many other people sell major appliances requires you to develop as many "points of difference" as you can to set you apart from the competition. Sometimes the only point of difference you have is your logo and your slogan.

5. CUT COPY

Once copy has been prepared by you or someone else, cut out every single word you possibly can without destroying the ad. The cleaner and quicker you can make your offer to your prospect, the better. If you are looking at an ad and you don't see anything you can cut, you are not doing your job.

Want some practice? Look at any ad in any newspaper for any product or service. Put a line through any sentence that does not impress you. You will be amazed at how advertisers blather on about things that you, the consumer, don't care anything about. The same thing will be true of your ads. Don't tax the reader any more than is necessary to get your message.

6. PREPARE F-A-R AHEAD OF DEADLINES

Don't do an ad today that has to go in the newspaper in two or three days. Get it done at least a week or two before the closing date so you can pick it up three or four times and review it before turning it over to the newspaper. You will be surprised at how often something looks good on first sight, and a day or two later, you find flaws or just plain errors.

7. USE ALL THE MEDIA

Don't limit your advertising to just radio or just newspapers. Try, over a period of time, to utilize all media: newspapers, radio, television and direct mail. There are some new people to be reached by every medium. And if you repeat your message to any one prospect by reaching him or her with more than one medium, so much the better.

8. NO "PICTURES OF THE FACTORY"

Avoid copy that talks about "years of research to bring you blah-blah ... ," and "state of the art" developments. Tell the prospect exactly what your "developments" are and *how they will benefit him*. Don't talk about the thousands of dollars you have spent to develop a new product. Nobody cares.

9. WORK YOUR REFERRALS

Believe it or not, many businesses could double their volume if they had a system for working referrals. A satisfied customer is your best source of new business—even better than advertising. Develop a system which rewards a satisfied customer for providing you with a new customer.

If your advertising cost you $10 for a new customer, why not give a satisfied customer $5 if she supplies a new customer? It's cheaper than advertising. As a consumer, you know that few businesses do this. Why they don't do it can be answered by one word: stupidity!

10. KEEP IT GOING

I've saved the most important commandment for last. Keep a regular advertising program going. There will be times when you feel you simply must save the money for a month or so. Resist this temptation. A continuing advertising program anchors you to the community as a substantial business, and there are many prospects who will react to your advertising the tenth or twentieth time they see it and not before.

The very month you decide to take a break from advertising will be a month when more than one prospect will need a product or service like yours. Don't throw away the chance to reach them when their need is greatest.

Your advertising program is as much a part of your total marketing effort as your legs are part of your body. Of course you can function with one leg or even with no legs, but you want to do everything you can to avoid putting yourself in that position.

KEEP IT GOING!

Index

A/S ratio, definition, 4
Acting in your own radio and television ads, 57-58
Ad size selection, for writing, 109
Advertising as art, not science, 1-2
Advertising, why do it, 2-3
Affiliated newspapers, 38
Agate lines, 34
Agency commissions, radio and television, 52
Agency contract, what it should say, 25
Agency, advertising: how it gets paid, 20-21; what it does, 20
Agency, direct mail, selecting, 67
Agency, finding a good, 24-25
Agency, media as, 26ff
Agency-client relationship, 23
Animation in radio and television commercials, 61
Art department, newspaper, 27
Asking for the order, ad writing, 112
Audience, radio and television, 53

Bold listings, yellow pages, 84
Borders, newspaper ad, 42-44, 45
Budget forms, sample, 95-96
Budget, direct mail, 70
Budgeting for advertising, 91ff
Bulk mail permit, 75

Business cards, using to build sales, 12
Business growth, and advertising, 6

Cable penetration, 54
Cable television, 54-55
Cash with order, as ad agency payment, 21
Category choosing, yellow pages, 83
Charges for newspaper ad preparation, 29
Claims in advertising, 100-101
Closing dates, newspaper, 38-39
Closing deadlines, radio and television, 51-52
Co-op advertising, 78ff
Color ads in yellow pages, 83
Color, using in direct mail, 71
Combination rates, newspaper, 36-37
Combined newspapers, 38
Commercials, creating radio and television, 56-57
Commercials, radio and television, humor in, 59
Commission, ad agency, 22-23; negotiating, 24
Competitive advertising, 97-98
Competitive material, reviewing for ad writing, 108-109
Competitive protection for newspaper inserts, 47

Competitive protection, radio
and television, 51
Computerized production of
radio and television
commercials, 61-62
Contests, as public relations, 18
Continuing advertising, 93
Contract, newspaper ad, 35
Contract, with ad agency, 25
Copy research, 8; rules of, 9-10
Copy, writing body, 111-112
Copy, writing finished, 113-114
Costs, direct mail, 75-76
Costs, of newspaper ads, 32-33
Coupon format, direct response,
64
Cume (cumulative audience), 53
Cumulative effect of
advertising, 106-107
Customer referrals, 12

Direct mail advertising, 67ff
Direct mail, how it works and
where to start, 68
Direct mail lists, 69
Direct response advertising, 63-
64
Discount coupon books, 88-90
Discount offers, direct response,
66
Discounts for newspaper ads, 35
Dumb heroines, in commercials,
60

Effectiveness of advertising, 98,
105-107
Effectiveness of transit ads, 87
Failures, common, in ad copy, 8-
9
Fourth quarter in radio and
television, 62

Freelance writers and producers,
radio and television, 57

Goal of book, 1
Gutter, position of newspaper ad
in, 40

Headline writing, 109-111
HUT (homes using television),
53

In-store co-op advertising, 78-79
Inserts, newspaper, 44, 46;
competitive protection for, 47;
cost of, 47; benefits, 48
Inside/outside transit
advertising, 86-87

Leading, newspaper ad, 42-43
Logo, creating, using and
contracting for, 102-103

Mailing list building, direct
response, 65
Mailing lists, direct mail, 69
Mailing pieces, folded, direct
mail, 72
Marketing and sales mix,
advertising as part of, 4-5
Me too advertising, 99-100
Measuring newspaper ad size, 34
Media as ad agency, 26ff
Multimedia advertising, 98-99
Multiple listings, yellow pages,
84
Music in radio and television
commercials, 60-61

Negotiating rates, radio and
television, 50, 51
New ads, don't do, 98

Newspaper ad layouts, 27-29
Newspaper ad rates, 32-34
Newspaper advertising, 32ff
Newspaper co-op advertising 79
Newspaper, as ad agency, 26ff

Operating budget, advertising
   as recommended percentage of,
Out-of-home radio listeners, 55

Paid position of newspaper ad,
   39-40
Paper weight, direct mail, 72
Paying for yellow pages ads, 82
Photo reproduction, newspaper,
   29
Picture of the factory
   advertising, 101
Picture, need for in print ads,
   112-113
Placement of newspaper ad (see
   Position)
Planning ahead, yellow pages,
   80-81
Pop lingo, 101-102
Position of newspaper ad, 39-40
Postcard, direct mail, 71, 73
Preemptable rates, radio and
   television, 50
Press releases, 13ff
Printing transit ads, 86
Promotional advertising, 93
Public relations firms, 11
Public relations, doing it
   yourself, 12, 18
Public service organizations,
   public relations and fund
   raising for, 18

Radio and television
   advertising, 49ff

Radio and television direct
   response, 65-66
Radio and television
   promotions, 19
Radio and television, choosing
   stations, 54
Radio and television, surveying
   audiences for, 55
Radio station as agency, 30
Rate card, newspaper, 32-33
Rate cards, radio and
   television, 49-50
Rate holders, newspaper, 37-38
Ratings, radio and television, 52
Repro, newspaper ad, 29
Response pattern, direct
   response advertising, 63
Response rates, direct mail, 76
Retainer, as ad agency payment,
   21-22
Return cards, direct mail, 74
Return mail permits, 74
Reverse printing, newspaper ad,
   41-42
Right-hand page, position of
   newspaper ad, 40
ROP (run of press), 39-40

Screening, newspaper ad, 42
Self-liquidating advertising, 90
Self-mailers, direct mail, 72-73
Service columns in newspapers,
   12-13
Share, radio and television, 53
Short rate, newspaper, 35-36
Showings, transit ad, 86
Signature, ad writing, 112
SIU (sets in use), 53
Sizes of yellow pages ads, 81-82
Slicks, newspaper ad, 29
Slogan, importance of, 104

Teaser advertising, 102
Telephone number, giving in
 direct response radio and
 television ads, 66
Television station as ad agency,
 30-31
Ten commandments of
 advertising, 116-119
Testimonials, radio and
 television, 59

Transit advertising, 85ff
TV Guide rates, 1

Value of yellow pages
 advertising, 82-83

White space, newspaper ad, 44
Writing an ad, 108-115

Yellow pages advertising, 80ff